Once upon a time,

a young wizard's apprentice named Jaimie joined the master wizard, Pentegarn, in a war of wizards at Rainbow Castle. YOU are Jaimie and you control your own fate. Tricked into leaving Pentegarn's side, you must battle strange monsters and magical creatures in order to save you and your friends from almost certain death in the tunnels and towers of the magical castle.

What will you do?
Forced into a tower high in the castle, you must choose from several dangerous paths to win your way to freedom.

1) If you want to try to climb down the outside of the tower, turn to page 12.

2) If you want to go down the hidden staircase into the unknown, turn to page 105.

3) If you decide to fight the three-headed dog blocking the door, turn to page 8.

Whichever path you pick, you are sure to find adventure, as you turn the pages of
REVENGE OF THE RAINBOW DRAGONS

An ENDLESS QUEST™ Book #6

REVENGE of the RAINBOW DRAGONS

Cover Art by Jeff Easley
Interior Art by Harry Quinn

TSR Hobbies, Inc.

This book is for Jim Ward,
whose friendship and ideas have enriched my life.

Also by Rose Estes and published by TSR Hobbies, Inc.:

DUNGEON OF DREAD
MOUNTAIN OF MIRRORS
PILLARS OF PENTEGARN
RETURN TO BROOKMERE
REVOLT OF THE DWARVES

Distributed to the book trade in the United States by Random House, Inc. and in Canada by Random House of Canada, Ltd.
Distributed in the United Kingdom by TSR (UK) Ltd.
Distributed to the toy and hobby trade by regional distributors.

DUNGEONS & DRAGONS & ENDLESS QUEST are trademarks owned by TSR Hobbies, Inc.

D&D is a registered trademark owned by TSR Hobbies, Inc.

First Printing: January, 1983   Second Printing — April 1983
Printed in the United States of America
Library of Congress Catalog Card Number: 82-51206
ISBN: 0-88038-021-7

9 8 7 6 5 4 3 2

All characters in this book are fictitious. Any resemblance to actual persons, living or dead, is purely coincidental.

TSR Hobbies, Inc.
POB 756
Lake Geneva, WI 53147

TSR Hobbies (UK) Ltd.
The Mill, Rathmore Road
Cambridge CB1 4AD
United Kingdom

oxes aren't supposed to fly, Jaimie," Fox says nervously, as he hovers in midair. "How about putting me down? Leave the flying to Featherface. I feel better on old terra extra-firma."

"Hush, Friend Fox," scolds Pentegarn. "Consider yourself part of an important lesson. This is the first time Jaimie has levitated an object. And you know he needs silence to concentrate."

"Now I'm an object," mutters Fox in disgust, as he dangles above the ground.

You ache with the effort of holding the spell. Just as you feel you are mastering the skill, a thunderous noise rolls through the room. Your concentration breaks and Fox falls to the floor with a thump.

"Oh, Fox, I'm sorry," you cry, rushing to his side. "I'll be more careful next time."

"Next time?" growls Fox. "Forget it! I have to go dig a den—a very long one." He turns and trots quickly from the room.

"Unfortunate attitude," says Owl. "But what can one expect from the family Canidae?"

"Well done, child," says Pentegarn. "You're moving ahead nicely with your studies. I hadn't planned on your being able to lift objects for another six months or so. But now that we've been interrupted, I suppose we'd better see who's at the door." And he makes a small gesture with his hand.

Poof! A cloud of dust appears, then clears. Before you stands a travel-stained man, one hand raised as if knocking on a door.

Lowering his hand, the traveler snaps, "Do you always answer doors like that? But then, what else should I expect from a wizard?" Giving a short bow, he says, "Sir, I come from Rainbow Castle. Your presence is required, no later than four days hence."

"Is it a party?" you ask hopefully.

The messenger fixes you with an icy glance. "Hardly. You will answer to charges of occupying the Castle of the Pillars and calling yourselves 'Wizard and Apprentice.' This castle is part of the domain assigned to the wizards Malus, Pothos, and Rubus. Unless you can support your claim to the castle and win their permission to practice wizardry in the area, you will be banished from this land," says the messenger coldly. "And now, if you will show me the door, I will return to Rainbow Castle."

Poof! A cloud of smoke forms in front of the messenger, and when it clears, a large wooden door stands before him.

"A mere first-level spell," sneers the messenger. "You'll have to do better than that at Rainbow Castle." Still sneering, he turns and strides out of the room.

"Rainbow Castle? Wizards? What's this all about, sir?" you ask worriedly.

"Centuries ago, when I lost my kingdom to the Evil One, Rainbow Castle was in the hands of the forces of good," sighs Pentegarn, "and the three brothers Malus, Pothos, and Rubus were apprenticed to a third-rate wizard. Obviously, while I was in the Evil One's power, the balance changed. I think we had better meet with them. It is always best to be polite to one's neighbors."

"I think I'll sit this one out," says Fox, poking his head through the doorway. "That fellow didn't look too pleasant, and he's only the messenger."

"Pshaw!" says Owl. "Don't be such a coward. Remember: Cowards die a thousand deaths. The valiant die but once."

"Go feather a nest, Beak Brain," growls Fox.

"We will let Jaimie decide. As my apprentice and the heir to this kingdom, Jaimie must learn to make good, sound decisions," says Pentegarn. And suddenly there are three pairs of eyes staring at you.

"Well," you stammer, thinking quickly, "the way I see it, we have only two choices:

1) "Go to Rainbow Castle and see if we can work out our problems with our neighbors." Turn to page 110.

2) "Ignore them and don't go." Turn to page 83.

"I don't like the idea of climbing down from this tower," you say. "High places make me dizzy. And that fireplace stairway must be a trap. Otherwise we wouldn't have found it so easily. I have an idea! Let's fight that creature—or rather, let's trick it."

Still concentrating on keeping the spiders up on the ceiling, you back up behind the door and motion Fox and Owl to join you. "Be ready to move—fast!—when I give you the word." And you open the door quickly.

Snapping, snarling jaws snatch at you as the three-headed dog bursts into the room. At the instant you open the door, you drop your concentration, ending the levitation spell. Before the dog can even reach you, it is covered by the rug full of spiders. Shrieking in fear and pain, the dog falls to the floor and rolls over and over, trying to shake off the spiders.

It does no good. Gradually, its agonized thrashing grows slower and slower and then ceases. Instantly, the spiders begin to spin, and within seconds, the awful three-headed dog is completely encased in spider silk.

"Kid, I hate to interrupt the show, but don't you think we should leave before they decide we'd make a nice dessert?" asks Fox.

Even as he speaks, a few spiders leave the dog and move toward you. Jolted into action, you yell loudly and the three of you race through the door and slam it.

You pound down a narrow, winding stairway, wild with relief at escaping the spiders,

the dog, and the room—until Owl perches on your shoulder and says, "Perhaps a more moderate pace would be indicated by the multitude of dangers we have encountered in such a short span of time."

"I think he means slow down, Jaimie," says Fox. "It's not a bad idea." Turning to Owl, he says, "If we ever get out of here, I'm going to press you between the pages of the biggest dictionary I can find. You can learn some simple words there!"

Your heart is pounding and your knees are wobbly, but you can't help laughing at Fox's words. Weakly you sink to the step and lean against the cold stone wall.

Just as you are about to speak, you hear an eerie howl coming from somewhere ahead of you—a howl that sends chills up and down your spine. You huddle up against the wall and, to your amazement, it moves beneath your touch. An opening appears.

"OOOOOOOO!" wails the creepy howl.

"It would appear that something this way comes," says Owl.

1) If you want to find out what is making the awful noise, turn to page 49.

2) If you want to slip into the open space in the wall, turn to page 76.

"I don't think they should go," you say. "I mean, there's so many of them. Why don't they stay here and we'll come back for them later?"

"NO!" cries Quentin, and before you can say another word, he grabs you by the neck and flings you into a small stone room. Fox and Owl follow you with a thump and a crash, and the door closes firmly behind them.

"I thought you understood," yells Quentin as he stomps away. "But you're just like all the others! Mushrooms have rights too!"

"Good going, kid," growls Fox. "Have you ever thought of being a diplomat?"

The three of you sit and stare at each other. You are all covered with smears of the glowing fungus. Lighting your own way, you explore the tiny room.

"We must hope that our captors are mushrooms of honor and that they mean well and will return for us," says Owl. "I suggest that we entwine our metacarpals and pray."

And so you sit, glowing in the dark, with claws, paws, and fingers crossed, hoping that this is not

THE END

Fighting the cold, blowing wind and rain, you squeeze through the narrow window. Behind you, you hear the rug drop and the plop, plop, plop of falling spiders.

"Do me a favor, kid—don't fall, huh," quavers Fox from inside your shirt. "I'm too gorgeous to become a grease spot."

"Don't worry, Fox. I don't want to fall either."

As you clutch the tough stems of the ivy, you shout to Owl, who flaps near your shoulder. "At least we don't have to worry about those wizards. They can't get us up here."

"Hold fast, youngster," calls Owl. "We are about to be engulfed by a large cloud."

You turn in time to see a large mass of pinkish stuff close in on you, and then you see nothing. You bury your face against the crispness of the vine, its bark rough beneath your fingers, hoping that the cloud will pass quickly. Fox scrambles out of your shirt and disappears into the mist.

And then a strange thing happens—you no longer feel the shrubbery, and the comforting solidity of the vine fades from your grasp. It feels as if you were drifting away on a misty cloud.

Please turn to page 69.

You continue urging Pentegarn to wake up, while concentrating on the spell. Just as you are beginning to despair, Pentegarn moves.

"Hooray! He's waking up!" yips Fox joyfully.

All at once, a brilliant light floods the dark room. You hear screams of anguish and terror.

Opening your eyes, you see confusion. Owl flies about the room, dipping and wheeling, looking for an enemy who has vanished.

Imogene screams and hollers and stamps her feet in rage, crying, "They're gone! They're gone! And now I'll never know!"

Turning in wonder to Pentegarn, now upright and alert, you notice that he holds on his outstretched palm the Cube of Mystic Forces. It sits serene, crystal clear, and glowing with a strange warmth. Inside the cube, hands and faces pressed desperately against its clear surfaces, are the three evil wizards.

Eyes open wide, you stare at the tiny figures. "Wow! How did you do that?"

"You'll learn some day, Jaimie, when you have the wisdom to handle such power," says Pentegarn, placing his arm around you.

"Where are they? What have you done with them?" screeches a shrill voice, and suddenly Pentegarn gasps and clutches his ankle.

"Imogene, don't! This is Pentegarn, my great-grandfather! He's a powerful wizard and a good guy!"

"What's he done with my rotten uncles?" screeches Imogene. "I've got to find out where my father is!"

"Here they are," says Pentegarn, holding out the cube, "and I'll find out the answer to that question if you promise not to kick me again."

Imogene's face turns a deep, dark red and her foot trembles, but at last she mutters, "All right, but find out fast!"

Pentegarn places the cube against his forehead and closes his eyes. Instantly a bright yellow glow surrounds the cube and the tiny figures inside sag limply.

Seconds later, Pentegarn lowers the cube and smiles. "There, that wasn't hard. Your father is in the dungeons, my dear, and we'll rescue him in a minute. But first, what shall we do with these fellows?"

"Stamp on them!" shrills Imogene. "No, wait!" An evil grin crosses her face. "Can we send them anywhere I want and make sure they can't get back?"

"Certainly," says Pentegarn. "As long as they can do no harm to anyone else."

"Don't worry, they'll be the ones in danger—from each other," smiles Imogene slyly. "Let's send them back up to Limbo and put them where they put me. It'll serve them right!"

"Done!" says Pentegarn, and placing the cube to his forehead once more, he closes his eyes. The cube turns pink and then slowly pales, becoming clear. And then it is totally empty.

"Wow!" you breathe in awe.

"How come they got you, Pentegarn? I figured you could take those guys with one hand tied behind your back," says Fox.

"They cheated, my furry friend. They brought a powerful magical amulet into the contest. Against it, I was helpless. And without your timely help, I would have been lost. You have my everlasting thanks."

"It was nothing," says Owl.

"Sure it was! It was quick, brilliant thinking and brave action on my part," growls Fox. "Speak for yourself, Bird Brain."

"And now that we have solved the question of who has the right to practice magic, I suggest we bid farewell to Rainbow Castle and return home," says Pentegarn.

"AFTER we find my father," demands Imogene, lifting her foot in a threatening manner.

"And maybe, after we get home, I can learn to do something besides levitate," you say. "If things keep going like this, I'm going to need it."

THE END

"If these guys scare US—and we're kind of used to them—imagine how those wizards upstairs will feel," snickers Fox.

"The element of surprise would indeed be useful," adds Owl.

"All right, we'll all go," you say.

"Let's get ready then. The messenger should be here soon," says Quentin.

The mushroom men hide themselves in another corridor, and you, Fox, Owl, and Quentin crouch beside the cave entrance, waiting quietly.

Soon you hear footsteps hurrying toward you, and a figure passes through the doorway. Instantly, all of you fling yourselves upon the figure and bring him crashing to the ground.

A muffled snarl erupts from beneath you. "You dare lay hands upon a wizard's official messenger?"

"We'll lay more than hands on you if you don't cooperate," snarls Fox, showing his long white fangs.

"I won't do it, whatever it is you want. And no matter how you threaten or bribe me, I won't show you the way out of here."

"Well, if you won't show us, I guess you'll just have to stay here," says Quentin with a nasty smile. Pulling the necklace out of his pocket with a quick motion, he places it around the messenger's neck and forces the broken ends together.

"There! I can't think of anyone who deserves it more, except perhaps my beloved uncles. Enjoy your stay here. I hope you like mushrooms."

The messenger stands dazed for a moment and then, before your eyes, begins to change shape. Soon, thickened and mushroomlike, he wanders aimlessly off into the dark.

"Wonderful. Now what do we do?" asks Fox.

1) "I know," you say. "Quentin, do you have any more of those homing bats? We could tie a string on its leg and follow it." Turn to page 106.

2) "Or maybe I could find a way out by sniffing," says Fox. "If Mouse Breath would help, I think we could do it." Turn to page 144.

"Look, are we going to let a little noise scare us away?" you ask angrily.

"Sounds good to me. I want to get out of here," says Fox, starting down the stairs.

"I agree with Jaimie," says Owl. "I should like to check out this curiosity. Let's find out what produces such a great and steady volume of noise."

"Two against one, Fox," you say, and Owl flies up, plucks the key from its hook, and places it in your hand.

With trembling hands, you place the heavy key in the lock, and the screaming stops.

"You'll excuse me if I stay down here," says Fox, crouching on the second step with only his nose, eyes, and ears visible.

You turn the key in the lock, ready for the worst—a whirlwind of magic, a horrible monster, a frightening vision.

The door opens and you see a pink blur of motion and feel a sharp pain in your ankle. You clutch the wounded ankle with both hands and hop up and down with pain.

"What took you so long?" screams a harsh, ugly voice. "Why didn't you come up here right away and let me out? You, you, slug!"

"Ow! Ow! Stop kicking me! Who are you? What are you doing here?"

"I'm a princess, dummy! Princess Imogene!" screams the little girl. "It certainly took you long enough to rescue me!" And she kicks you again, this time in the other leg.

"Ow! Stop that! How could I rescue you

sooner? I didn't even know you were here and needed rescuing. How did you get here?"

"I don't know," wails the little girl. "My uncle brought me here. He said there was something he wanted me to see, a surprise. He sent me up the stairs and I came in the room, and the door slammed shut behind me. And... and I've been here ever since," Imogene says, bursting into tears.

As she cries, you peer into the room. You see a small bed, a nightstand, and the broken bodies of hundreds of dolls and toys.

"Don't cry," you say, patting Imogene on the head. "We're here now. We'll get you out."

"Don't touch me!" screams Imogene. "How dare you, a commoner, touch a princess without permission!"

"Look, Imogene," you say, "I'm sorry if I don't come up to your royal standards. But just remember—I AM rescuing you. If that's not good enough, go back in your room and wait for a royal prince to come."

"I vote for that," growls Fox. "Put her back in her room, the graveyard of the dolls. If we let her out, she'll probably break us into little bits too."

"What is that mangy dog doing in my castle?" screams Imogene. "Get rid of it immediately. It clashes with my dress."

You notice for the first time that Imogene is dressed entirely in pink. Long curls flow over her shoulders and freckles are sprinkled over her frowning face.

"Mangy dog?" snarls Fox with menace.

"Now, now, Fox. Control yourself," says Owl from his place on your shoulder. "Just consider this child as ill-tempered and simple, not worldly and well-mannered like yourself."

"Well, since you put it that way," says Fox, sinking back on his haunches. "But we should vote and decide what to do with her."

"You? A commoner and two dirty animals decide what to do with me?" screams Imogene, with her hands on her hips.

"We three are a democracy, Imogene. We make all important decisions by voting, and the majority rules. Fox and Owl may only be animals to you, but they are my best friends and I value their opinions."

"Hmmph!" sniffs Imogene.

"Well, let's put it to a vote," you say. As you speak, Fox leaves the safety of the steps and sits at your feet.

1) "Should we take her along with us?" Turn to page 53.

2) "Or should we leave her here and go on by ourselves?" "If you do that you'll be very sorry," screeches Imogene. If this is your choice, turn to page 89.

You go on but fear that you have made the wrong decision. Just as you are about to suggest turning around and going back, you see a glimmer of light ahead of you.

"Look up ahead. It's a light! Hurry!" you cry, urging your friends forward.

The light dances and floats in front of you. You run toward the glow, pulling Nesbitt behind you. He shouts vague words, but you do not stop to listen.

The light moves into another tunnel, and you follow without a second thought. "Hurry! We'll be out soon!" you yell. The light turns again and still you follow.

Somehow, no matter how fast you run, you never catch up to the moving light. It turns many corners and changes its direction often. But it is always just out of reach.

At last you can follow no longer. You sink to the floor in despair. The light stops and bobs up and down gently . . . waiting.

"It's no use. It's a Will-o'-the-Wisp," gasps Nesbitt. "It has no intelligence. It leads nowhere. We are lost forever."

"No! We're not lost! Use your stones!"

"I cannot. I dropped them. I tried to tell you, but you did not listen."

A silence sinks over your party as each of you realizes that you are truly lost. And in the distance, the Will-o'-the-Wisp bobs up and down . . . and waits.

THE END

"No, it couldn't be. It's got to be just a plain old ring," you say, looking at it.

Suddenly your eyes open wide. What you saw before as bright metal is now dull and gray—nothing more than a circle of poorly forged iron. It turns to grainy powder and crumbles to dust even as you watch.

"Besides, if it had been a wish ring, the fourth wish would have canceled out everything I wished before. And I sure don't want these guys on us again," you say with a shudder.

Settling on your shoulder, Owl says, "I see an exit at the end of this room."

Kicking away the last of your tiny pursuers, the three of you slip through the door and close it behind you.

"Wow! We're safe," you say breathlessly.

"Oh, yeah? What makes you say that, kid? We're still lost. We're still in the dark. Why can't we ever get lost in daylight?"

"Some of us are more in the dark than others," murmurs Owl.

"I know just what you mean, Fox," you say quickly. "But here, I guess I can fix it for a while." Holding out your hand, you utter magical words that have never been more than boring homework before. A glowing ball appears in front of you, casting light ten feet in all directions.

"When did you learn that? And why didn't you use it before this?" sputters Fox.

"I was saving this until we really needed it.

And we need to get back to Pentegarn. The light will help."

Avoiding further quarrel, you walk down the corridor revealed by the light.

Faded tapestries and formal portraits line the stone walls. Underfoot, a fine carpet lies buried by thick dust.

You open every door you pass, but each reveals only an empty, lifeless room.

The glowing ball sputters and fizzes, glows its last, and disappears. In its dying light you reach the last door in the corridor. With shaking hand, you grasp the doorknob and push. The door creaks open and bright sunlight streams into the dark corridor. With your hand over your dazzled eyes, you enter the most splendid room you have ever seen.

Bright, warm light streams in through three rounded tower windows. On the floor is a thick carpet patterned in flowers of vivid red, blue, gold, and green that wriggle aside as you pass. On the walls hang richly colored and intricate tapestries.

More books than you have ever seen before spill out of bookcases, cascade off chairs and tables, and overflow onto the floor.

The door closes quietly behind you. Out from behind a chair come two large comfortable-looking slippers. Flip, flop, flip, flop go the slippers as they pad up to you and arrange themselves on either side of your feet. When you do not move, they jump up and down with a demanding thump.

With a sidelong look at Fox and Owl, you step out of your own boots and into the big slippers, which promptly stride across the room, taking you with them.

"Be careful!" barks Fox. "Those things could be a trap."

But the slippers walk to a large overstuffed chair, turn themselves around, and back you into the seat, settling you deep in its soft, sagging depths.

As you sit there, your legs dangling over the edge, a large curved wooden pipe on the table next to you stands up. A round wooden canister opens itself up, releasing a sweet smell into the air. A chunk of tobacco floats through the air and packs itself into the bowl of the pipe. Instantly, a roaring fire bursts into life across the room. A spark leaps from it, flies to the pipe, and settles into the tobacco. Great puffs of smoke soon billow out of the bowl as the pipe lights itself.

The smoking pipe floats through the air and places itself firmly between your lips. You inhale in surprise, and thick, harsh smoke pours down your throat. "Get me something to drink," you gasp, coughing.

Even before you have finished speaking, a long-stemmed glass thrusts itself into your hand. Not questioning where the glass came from or what it contains, you raise it to your lips and swallow deeply.

Hot, raging, burning fire courses down your throat and settles like a pool of lava in your stomach. Tears pour down your cheeks and you are sure you'll never breathe again. Then a soothing pressure pats you firmly on the back and rubs gently between your shoulder blades.

At last your harsh coughing dies, and you are not even startled when a soft, knitted afghan lifts itself from a nearby hook and wraps itself comfortingly around you.

"What is this stuff?" says Fox, lapping at the amber liquid in the glass.

"I will determine its chemical elements," says Owl, dipping his beak into the glass.

"Hmmmmmm, unusual flavor," adds Fox. "I think I'd better try that again. It might be poison." Dipping his muzzle into the glass again, he slurps up more of the fluid.

"I am better at distinguishing among the many complex chemical compounds than you are. Make way for the expert," says Owl, drinking deeply.

As you snuggle in the depths of the large chair, trying to sort out confused thoughts, Fox turns to Owl and says, "Old Buddy, did I ever tell you that even though you can be a real pain, you're not so bad for a bird?"

"And I have frequently thought that, hic, for a member of the genus Canis, you are rather exceptional yourself. Hic."

"Say, do you know that old song that the Wood Elves, hic, Wood Elves sing?"

"Hummmm a few bars, friend Fox," says Owl, blearily.

By the tree and by the root
We really love to drink this fruit.
Sharing's nice, it's really fine!
But give me more, or I'll take thine.

"Fine tenor voice, Fox. I myself sing bari-tone," says Owl, sagging comfortably against a pile of books. And the two of them raise their voices in silly song.

As the pain in your throat and chest eases, you sit up straighter in the chair just in time to grab a very large book that settles itself in your lap and opens to a well-used page. Gold letters heaped in one corner march them-selves quickly across the page and arrange themselves into lines of words.

As you try to understand the words, your friends' voices turn quarrelsome.

"That was my chorus, you Buzzard, you! You should stick to hooting."

"Howling at the moon is more your tune," snipes Owl.

"That does it! That's the final straw. I'll show you who's going to howl," shrieks Fox as he leaps upon Owl.

Fur and feathers fly in a frantic flurry of beak and tooth, claw and talon. Then Fox snaps at Owl, catches him by the back of the neck, and drags him across the room.

Stopping in front of an enormous open book, Fox drags a struggling, flapping Owl up into the book, wedges him into it, and slams the cover shut.

"There! I told you I'd do this. Now! While you're in there, learn some simple words or I'll never, ever let you out!"

"Mfle! Pring!" squeaks Owl from between the pages of the dictionary.

Fox sits on top of the heavy book with a satisfied smirk on his face, wraps his tail around his legs, and settles down for a long, satisfying wait.

You start to rise, but the strange words that have formed on your page demand your attention. And you realize that Fox and Owl must settle their own differences if there is ever to be peace.

Before you on the large page are three blocks of words. One reads: "How to Rescue a Friend." The second reads: "How to Be Wise." The third reads: "How to Be Powerful."

Each has a magical formula written beneath it that you know you could figure out with a little effort.

1) If you want to read the spell that says "Rescue a Friend," turn to page 100.

2) If you want to read the spell that says "Be Wise," turn to page 135.

3) If you want to read the spell that says "Be Powerful," turn to page 121.

"He'll never wake up in time. If we're to be saved, I'd better try to use the cube myself," you say nervously.

"No! Jaimie! You haven't enough experience to use it yet," squawks Owl.

"Pentegarn won't wake up. I have to try," you say, raising the cube to your forehead the way you have seen Pentegarn do.

A mighty surge of power zaps into your head and flows down through your body. You are rigid with shock. Your thoughts whirl through your mind like birds in a storm, but they are the only things that move.

You are unable to move even your little finger. Through frozen eyes you see the wizards untangle themselves from their robes and move toward you.

Malus plucks the cube from your nerveless fingers. "A fine addition to our collection of magical goodies, wouldn't you say, Pothos? Good thing the brat decided to use it or it would have been all over for us.

"Now I suppose we had best herd the zoo and Pentegarn—and Imogene, mustn't forget Imogene—and lock them up in the dungeon. This one," he adds, tapping your rigid arm, "will do for a statue in the fountain.

"Yes, I'd say everything worked out for the best . . . for us."

THE END

"What happened? Where are we?" wails Fox, opening his eyes.

"We are in a narrow corridor dripping with slime and foul fluids. It appears to be the home of numerous tasty rats," answers Owl. "Wait! Here's a sign tacked on the wall. It says, 'Welcome to the Game Room.'"

You peer into the blackness surrounding you and groan. "Some game room! This is a dungeon! Those wizards tricked us. So they must be planning to trick Pentegarn. We've got to get out of here fast and get back to help him!"

"Easier said than done," says Owl.

"Ahwooo!" wails Fox, and the noise echoes through the darkness.

"Be quiet, Fox!" you yell, grabbing him and holding his muzzle shut. "None of us wants to be here, but until we figure out exactly where we are, we can't figure how to get out. And don't forget, there are usually all sorts of dangerous monsters and other creepy things wandering around in these old dungeons. So be quiet unless you want to be dinner for one of them," you add sternly.

"Right now the most important thing to do is to figure out how we're going to get out of here. Do you pick up any clues with your special senses?" you ask the animals.

"As a matter of fact, I have spied a most peculiar rainbow-colored cord that appears to be attached to the wall and gives off a faint glow," says Owl. "It stretches off to our left."

Cautiously you let go of Fox's muzzle, hoping that he will not start howling again. But he only lifts his nose into the air and sniffs.

"To our right I smell a strange, fungusy, foresty, earthy smell," says Fox. "And I hear something moving."

"Very good," you say. "Two clues. Well, which way should we go?"

1) If you want to follow the glowing rainbow cord, turn to page 43.

2) If you want to find out what is moving about and smelling earthy, turn to page 68.

"They scare me, Owl. Let's get out of here while we still have a chance."

With one last look at Fox, you start running, darting and weaving between the slow-moving figures. Arrows whiz by you. A mace narrowly misses your head, and once, Owl is creased by a spear. But at last you are clear of the grasping reach of the iron men.

On you run until you fear your lungs will burst. Gasping for breath, you hold your aching chest and collapse on the dusty floor.

"Owl, where do we go from here?"

"I don't know, young Jaimie. I fear that no matter where we go, it will no longer matter. We have lost our friend Fox. We have failed in our mission, and even worse, we have left the battlefield without our honor."

Somehow—you are never able to remember how—you find your way out of Rainbow Castle. Looking up at its great towers shrouded with mist, you realize that two of those you love best, Pentegarn and Fox, remain within its walls.

"I wish I had it to do over again, Owl. I sure would do it differently."

If you would like to make a
different choice and try again,
go back to page 82.

Raising your hand, you pound on the heavy door as hard as you can. The sound echoes in the distance, but no one comes. The shrill whining continues. Once again you pound on the door, but still no one answers. However, the noise changes tone.

"Well, now what do we do?" you ask.

Turn back to page 48
and make another choice.

"Nothing good lives in dungeons on purpose," you say. "Let's try to fight our way through them and head for that tunnel."

"Yeah! We'll show them," says Fox.

"I hope you are correct," says Owl, looking doubtful.

Drawing your dagger, you move swiftly toward the swaying shadows. As you near them, the smell grows stronger. It is strangely familiar, sort of like mushrooms.

Without pausing, you give a loud war cry and plunge your weapon into the first creature you meet—or try to. Your wrist is gripped and twisted, and your dagger falls to the floor.

You strike out with your other fist, and it, too, is grasped and held firmly. Then you are lifted off the ground and shaken hard. You hear barks of panic from Fox and one squawk from Owl—then all is silent.

"Have you caught them all?" asks an almost-human voice.

"Yes," answers a mealy, muffled voice.

"Good," says the human voice. "They certainly are an odd bunch, but it doesn't matter. As soon as they grow their gills and alter their shapes, they'll be just like the rest of you and won't cause any problems.

"Take them and give them their first dose of mushrooms."

Soft, spongy hands pull you forward. The smell of mushrooms is overpowering. You struggle but are held firm. Soon you find yourself being pushed into the mouth of the tunnel

you saw earlier. Fox and Owl and more lumpy creatures crowd in behind you.

Rich warm smells of cooking hang heavy on the air, and you realize how hungry you are.

"What are these things?" hisses Fox.

"I don't know," you answer. "Just be careful not to eat any of those mushrooms."

"I never drink or eat anything given to me by strangers," says Owl.

As you watch, one of the stumpy figures takes a stick and stirs the embers in a stone hearth. Bending, it scoops up an armload of coal and adds it to the glowing embers. Soon the room is lit by a bright fire. Hanging over the fire is a large iron pot that simmers and bubbles, sending good smells into the air.

But you can't take your eyes off the stumpy creatures revealed in the firelight. Although they are human in shape, their skin is rough and brown and lumpy. On what should be their necks are narrow openings that look like fish gills. Their heads are crude, shapeless lumps. Looking closely, you make out the suggestion of eyes, nose, and mouth on some of the creatures. But others have none at all. To your terrified eyes, the creatures look like nothing more than enormous walking mushrooms!

As you stare in terror, one of the creatures dips a bowl into the cooking pot, fills it, and walks toward you.

"Eat!" it commands, placing two more steaming bowls in front of Fox and Owl.

"You can't make us!" Fox barks bravely.

Chuckling, the creature says, "That is not necessary. You will be hungry soon and will eat. Then you will be just like us."

Turning, the mushroom people shuffle through the door. The last one through touches a lever and a grate of metal bars drops to the ground.

You rush to the grate and shake it, but it does not move. Slowly you return to Fox and Owl and look down at the stew. Good smells drift upward and your stomach rumbles its message of hunger.

"What do you think?" asks Fox. "Should we eat? Food can't really hurt us, can it?"

"I don't know, Fox. I just don't know."

Shaking your head, you wonder if your hunger will force you to eat, or if you will be able to hold out long enough to talk to the mushroom people and convince them to let you go.

THE END

"There's nothing wrong with being obvious," says Fox. "Let's try the door."

Hurriedly, you seize the doorknob and pull. Instantly a loud, crazed barking bursts forth, and a large brown dog with three horrible heads hurls itself at the opening.

Quickly, you slam the door shut and shiver with fear as it shakes beneath the frenzied attack of the dog.

"The rug! It's dropping!" shrieks Fox.

Snapping your attention back to the drooping, spider-filled carpet, you pin it to the ceiling once more.

"Fox," you whisper, "look out the window and see if we can climb down from here. Owl, check out the fireplace. See if there's any way to get out through there."

"We're up real high, Jaimie. I don't know if we could get down or not. But there's some kind of ivy growing all over the walls."

"There appears to be a hidden staircase on one side of this fireplace, which I can see with my superior eyesight," says Owl.

1) If you want to try to climb down the tower, turn to page 12.

2) If you want to try the hidden staircase, turn to page 105.

3) If you want to try to fight the dog, turn to page 8.

"Looks fine to me. I'm hungry. Let's eat. What could possibly happen?" growls Fox as he leaps to the top of the table. He sticks his muzzle into a large chocolate cake and begins to eat hungrily.

"Well, young one, one for all and all for one," says Owl, picking up a piece of candy and swallowing it whole.

"All right. I guess so, and anyhow it's too late now," you say as you pick up a glass of some pale pink liquid and take a long drink.

"See? That wasn't sooo...." says Fox as he fades and disappears from sight.

"Fox! Fox! Where aaaaare ..." cries Owl in alarm as he, too, disappears.

"Fox! Owl! Come back!" you cry. And then you feel soft, smooth, soothing warmth, and then nothing at all.

In the empty room, in the partially empty castle, a half-eaten chocolate cake becomes whole, a piece of candy arranges itself on a plate, and a half-empty glass refills itself. Then all is still, except for the thin, shrill noise that continues unheard.

THE END

The cord is velvety smooth to the touch. Although it glows with a soft, warm shimmery rainbow of colors, it sheds little real light. The darkness presses in on all sides.

"Where do you think it goes?" asks Fox.

"Let's go find out," you answer.

Holding the shining cord in one hand and your dagger in the other, you advance slowly.

"Do you see anything yet?" whispers Fox.

"I'm not sure. I think there's some sort of pinkish light up ahead," you answer.

"Correct," says Owl.

Cautiously you approach the light. Soon you make out a doorway filled with a dull pink glowing fog that seems almost solid. You cannot see through it. Oddly, the cord does not go through the door but continues down the dark corridor.

"What do we do now?" you ask.

1) "I hate this darkness. Let's go through the door," says Fox, dashing in. If you choose to follow, drop the cord and turn to page 69.

2) "I think we should follow the cord," says Owl. If this is your choice, turn to page 72.

Settling down in the dense cloud cover, you stare at the caves. All you can tell is that they are very large. A peculiar multicolored glow shimmers through the opening, but you do not know where it comes from or what could be making it.

"Why are we sitting here?" growls Fox. "Let's go down there and check it out!"

"No, let's wait. I'd like to see what lives in there before we have to face it."

Fox grumbles but does not argue.

You do not have long to wait. Around a thundercloud mountain come three of the most unusual dragons you have ever seen. Each is covered with scales that shimmer and glow and change colors before your astonished eyes.

The largest dragon is in the lead, holding a chunk of bright-blue substance in its jaws. Behind it, a slightly smaller dragon carries a mouthful of crimson red. Last of all is a small, delicate dragon who carries a little bundle of golden yellow.

With grace unusual for animals so large, the immense creatures flow smoothly through the air. The sun bathes them in light, sparkling on the multicolored scales and filtering through gauzy, transparent wings. With a gentle swirl, they bank and turn, enter the cave, and disappear into its depths.

"Wow! Will you look at that!" whistles Fox.

"Truly astonishing," murmurs Owl.

"I wouldn't have believed it if I hadn't seen

it," you say. "Well, what should we do? They look pretty nice to me. Not at all like dragons I've read about. They're so beautiful, maybe they're friendly. We could try to talk to them."

"Have you lost your grip? Are you nuts?" says Fox. "A dragon's a dragon! The only thing dragons understand is violence. Kill them, yes! Talk to them, no!"

"I myself attempt to avoid danger whenever possible. I suggest that we avoid this confrontation completely," says Owl.

1) If you want to try to talk to the dragons, turn to page 150.

2) If you want to fight the dragons, turn to page 65.

3) If you want to go to the cloud castle, go on to the next page.

"If there's a castle, there must be people who live in it and can help us. That's why I vote for the castle."

"I'm with you," says Fox, leaping to his feet and sinking to his belly in cloud.

"I second your decision," says Owl.

Although you can see little or nothing through the foggy mist, you move in the direction that Owl points out. With each step, you sink kneedeep in the clouds. The soft stuff wraps around your legs and tugs at your ankles. Soon your muscles ache and burn with the effort of moving.

Fox pants heavily as he struggles alongside you. "Have to stop for a minute," gasps Fox as he collapses.

"My keen sight tells me that the castle lies just beyond the next cloud field and up a slight hill. It's really not far. I think we should push on," urges Owl.

"That's easy for you to say, Beady Eyes. You're flying. Try walking. It's like trying to swim through glue. I don't think I can make it." Fox groans.

"Faint heart ne'er won . . . AAWWK!" Owl shrieks suddenly as Fox leaps up in the air and snaps at his tail. Owl flaps swiftly upward, narrowly avoiding the sharp, shiny teeth. With Fox in pursuit on the cloud below, he flies off toward the castle.

"I'll get you if it's the last thing I ever do," yelps Fox. "Then we'll see who's got a faint heart!"

Smiling, you heave yourself to your feet and struggle after the barking Fox.

At last you break out of the clinging cloud. A clean breeze blows softly about you. In front of you is a low hill. Perched on top is a small castle built of pink cloud puffs. Tiny slits of windows spiral up the sides of its towers. Heavy wooden doors are set into the castle wall.

Calling on your last reserve of strength, you climb to the top of the hill and collapse at the castle door.

"What took you so long?" asks Fox smugly. "We've been waiting for you for ages."

"Oh, I just thought I'd take my time and look at the scenery," you say, fighting down the impulse to strangle him.

As you stand before the massive doors, you hear a distant whining noise that sends chills down your back. "Well," you say, "somebody must be in there. But how do we get in?"

"I'd say we have three choices," says Owl.

1) "Knock on the door." Turn to page 36.

2) "Try to open it ourselves." Turn to page 132.

3) "Or find another way in." Turn to page 140.

"Listen, we're not going to let a little noise scare us, are we?" you ask.

"I don't know about you, kid, but I'm convinced we shouldn't go in there. That noise is REAL convincing! I want nothing to do with something that sounds that scary."

"Jaimie is right, Fox. Don't exhibit your cowardice," chirps Owl. "These sounds are merely ululations of vocal phonics, acting on your auditory sense in such a manner as to produce fear."

"OK, Owl, I admit it," screams Fox. "I AM scared. But that doesn't mean I'm dumb. And just because you can talk big words doesn't make you smarter or braver than me."

Still full of rage, Fox turns and stomps down the stairs. "You want action? You got it. Look out, noise, here I come!"

"Owl, I think you went too far," you say as you hurry to catch up with Fox. "You shouldn't tease him so much. Underneath all that wise-cracking, Fox is very sensitive, and he IS your friend."

"I was only pointing out his shortcomings so that he might endeavor to improve himself. However, I will try to be kinder in the future," agrees Owl.

"If there is a future," you mutter.

"OOOOOOOOOO!" wails the noise from around the very next turn in the stairs.

"Come on, you chickens," says Fox as he takes a deep breath and turns the corner. There is a sudden yelp and then silence.

Before your startled eyes, a misty white fox-shaped figure floats through the air and up the stairs toward you.

"Fox, a ghostly appearance is not appropriate at this time," Owl says sternly. "Whatever is making that noise could seize the opportunity to get us."

"Won't happen, Fuzzface. I've already been gotten. Thanks to you. But why don't we let bygones be bygones?" And so saying, Fox drapes a paw around Owl's neck.

PLINK! Owl seems to melt away beneath Fox's touch until his feathers fade to fog.

"Fox! Owl! Is this a joke? Don't do this to me. Come back!" you cry.

"OOOOOOOOO!" wail Owl and Fox together, as they drift close to you.

"Not bad, huh, kid? Maybe we could form a group. We could call it the Spiritones."

"What do you mean? Fox? Owl? What's happened to you? You're not ghosts, are you?" Fearfully you touch your friends.

PLINK! Your hand goes soft and strange. You hold it up and realize that you can see through it. The strange coolness spreads up your arm and soon engulfs your entire body.

"OOOOOOO!" you cry in fear.

"Don't worry, kid. We'll only haunt the best places," says Fox, and the three of you drift off down the stairs.

THE END

"It has been a while since I dined on spiders," says Owl, launching himself into the air. "They make tasty tidbits."

At first, it seems that Owl will succeed. He flies rapidly around the small room, snapping up spiders in midair. But for every one he eats, two more drop down. In a little while, he settles heavily on your shoulder.

"I don't believe I could even think about eating another bite."

"What do we do now, kid? There's more of them than there were before," says Fox nervously.

Turn back to page 138
and make another choice.

"Please take me with you," cries Imogene. "I'll try to be nice—really I will. Please don't leave me here by myself."

You look into the tear-stained, grubby face and for the first time see just a lost, frightened, unhappy little girl.

"I think we should take her," you say.

"Come, Fox. No true gentleman would leave a helpless female in distress," chides Owl.

"She's as helpless as an angry ogre," snorts Fox.

"Majority rules—Imogene comes with us."

"Good! I knew you'd see reason," says Imogene, wiping her face on a pink bedspread. "Now, let's get out of here."

"We'll regret this. Mark my words," says Fox glumly as you follow Imogene out of the room.

"Well, what's the plan?" asks Imogene as you sit on the doorstep of the cloud castle.

"What plan? We didn't plan to come here. We were tricked by some sneaky wizards."

"Me too!" exclaims Imogene in amazement.

"Maybe our wizards know your wizards," you say jokingly.

"I doubt it. No one goes to Rainbow Castle on purpose. My uncles are too nasty."

"Uncles?" asks Fox.

"Rainbow Castle?" asks Owl.

"Imogene," you say carefully. "Did you really come here from Rainbow Castle? Are Malus, Pothos, and Rubus really your uncles?"

"Why would I joke about that? They're my

father's uncles, actually. We were visiting them at Rainbow Castle, because it was my father's birthday and they invited us. I thought it was suspicious, but Daddy says I should be nicer. So we went. The next thing I knew, Daddy was gone and I was up in that crummy pink tower. I don't know what happened to Daddy, and I've been trying to get out of that stinking tower for ages."

"Hasn't anyone ever tried to rescue you?"

"Sure. Lots of people get sent here, but they either disappear or don't unlock the door. And as far as I'm concerned, there's no question of where we go. I want to go back to Rainbow Castle, find my father, and do something horrible to those uncles of mine."

"But how?" you ask with a sigh.

"My uncles are wizards, dummy, and I've learned a thing or two myself."

"But not enough to get out of that room," mutters Fox under his breath.

"I heard that, you ratty coyote."

Quickly you scoop Fox up, hold his jaws shut, and say, "Don't mind Fox, Imogene. He just has a hard time expressing himself. Please help us get back to Rainbow Castle."

"Mmf gurg!" gurgles Fox.

"Hmmff!" says Imogene. "Oh, very well. Everyone hold hands and close your eyes."

Fixing Fox with a warning look, you put him down. Forming a circle, you join hand to hand to wing to paw and close your eyes. And then the clouds and wind rush up about you.

There is a sudden feeling of weightlessness and falling. Then, a terrible thump.

Slowly you open your eyes. You are lying on the hard stone floor of Rainbow Castle.

"I did it!" exclaims Imogene, rising unsteadily to her feet.

"I may never move again," moans Fox.

"We couldn't be that lucky," says Owl.

"Get up!" says Imogene, poking you with her foot. "I want to find my uncles."

"But, Imogene, we can't! The rules were that we stay out."

"You dummy, do they keep the rules?" And turning, she walks straight to the doors of the Great Hall and flings them open.

Inside, the room is murky and dim. Blue bolts of electricity flash and shimmer.

You follow Imogene to the door and see Pentegarn lying senseless on the floor. Above him stand Malus, Pothos, and Rubus with nasty smiles on their faces.

Like a small pink whirlwind, Imogene attacks, kicking Pothos as hard as she can.

"Where's my father, you chubby creep?"

Pothos reels under the unexpected attack, trips over his robes, and falls to the floor. Instantly, Imogene falls upon the tubby wizard, kicking him as hard as she can.

Rubus and Malus watch their niece in horror until they see you approaching.

"Quick, Malus! Do something! That brat got back here somehow!" cries Rubus.

Malus lifts his hands and begins to point at

you. Then, out of the darkness zooms Owl, razor-sharp claws distracting the wizard.

You close your eyes and concentrate on doing the only thing you do well, levitate.

Instantly, the wizards' robes fly up and wrap around their heads. They stagger about blindly, trying to pull their robes down.

"Do something, Malus!" screams Rubus.

"I'm trying! I'm trying!" cries Malus, pointing at you. Blue fire pours from his fingertips and crackles above your head. Chunks of rock fall about you.

"Stop! You'll kill us!" screams Rubus.

Dodging, you rush to Pentegarn's side, keeping a tight mental hold on the spell.

"Fox, get his cube," you whisper. Then you shout, "Pentegarn, wake up. We need you!"

"Wha sa, whosis?" mumbles Pentegarn.

Fox returns, holding the Cube of Mystic Forces gently between his teeth.

"Pentegarn! Here's the cube. Use it!"

Your concentration begins to waver. It is becoming very difficult to hold the spell.

1) If you are afraid Pentegarn might not wake up in time, try to use the cube yourself, even though you don't know if you can control its powerful magic. Turn to page 32.

2) If you want to keep trying to wake Pentegarn up, so that he can use the cube, turn to page 13.

Bulky forms stop in front of you. Others circle behind you. You are surrounded.

"Greetings, dwellers of the deep," you say shakily. "Forgive our intrusion. We enter your domain unwillingly, victims of evil."

"What do you know of evil?" demands a deep voice, and the figures crowd closer.

"We have been tricked by three wizards who may, at this very moment, be murdering someone we love."

"These wizards, what are their names?"

"Malus, Pothos, and Rubus," you answer.

"SSSSSSSSsssssssss!" hiss the figures, and they begin to sway back and forth and stamp upon the ground with their large soft feet.

"Oh, boy! Now you've done it," whimpers Fox. "I knew this wouldn't work."

The hissing grows louder, and you gasp in fear as the largest figure steps forward.

"Who are you and how do you come to the land of the mushroom people?"

"Not on purpose, fella, that's for sure," says Fox, hiding behind your legs.

It does not take you long to tell your story and then there is silence for a time. Finally, the creature stirs and says, "Come with us," and walks off into the darkness.

The mushroom people march slowly on either side of you. A small cave opens to your left, and they gently herd you into it.

Lying on the floor is an enormous heap of mushrooms. Each is a different color and glows warmly.

A small fire burns under an iron kettle filled to the brim with a bubbling brew.

"Malus, Pothos, and Rubus!" exclaims the tall figure. "Still up to their evil tricks! If only they could be stopped. But how?"

"Excuse me, Mr. Mushroom, sir, but could you please tell me what's happening down here? Maybe if my friends and I knew more, we could help figure out what to do."

The figure utters a deep groan, and in a grief-filled voice says, "I was not always as you see me now. Much as I hate to admit it, I am nephew to those three wizards.

"My wicked uncles claimed this once-glorious castle as their own, using its powers for evil. One day a messenger appeared at my door bearing a note from my uncles. It said, 'Dear Quentin, We wish to repent of our evil ways. To convince you that we are sincere, we invite you to Rainbow Castle to celebrate your birthday. Please bring our beloved niece Imogene. Love, Your Uncles.'

"Imogene told me I was a fool, but I wanted to believe them.

"My uncles greeted us and, after a nice visit, presented me with this amulet."

Looking closely, you see a gold chain tightly circling the thick throat. Attached to the chain is a small gold mushroom.

"Shortly after I put it on, I found it difficult to breathe. It was almost as if I were being choked. I could not even swallow lunch, a mushroom stew made especially for my birthday. I touched my throat and felt it grow thick beneath my hand. I heard Imogene screaming. Then everything spun about me and I knew no more. When I woke up, the change was complete. I was a mushroom person.

"Now my friends and I tend the mushroom fields and make the hated shape-changing potion in return for the favors that those evil three give us to make our poor dark lives more bearable.

"I would do anything to leave the darkness of the dungeons and return to the sweetness of the open sky," groans Quentin.

"Well, what about the necklace thing?" asks Fox. "Sounds to me like all of your problems started when you put it on. Why don't you just take it off?"

"I can't. It won't come off."

"I wish I could help you, but I only know a few low-level spells."

"Can't you make the necklace larger, kid? Then he could just slip his head out of it."

"I don't know how, but I can do shrink spells."

"What good is that? You shrink his head small enough to get out of the necklace and he'll be a pinhead," objects Fox.

"I could shrink the necklace till it disappeared. No, then he'd be dead with his head chopped off."

"Great, kid! This stuff is real useful."

"I told you, I don't know a lot yet."

"Perhaps I can offer a suggestion," says

Quentin. "After all, I have a stake in this—it's my head. Can't you shrink just one link of the necklace? That would shatter it and I'd be free of the cursed thing!"

"Good idea! Let's try it." Concentrating hard, you place your finger on one tiny link in the gold chain and utter the magic words.

The link tightens, draws in upon itself, and snaps in two. And the necklace falls off.

"At last!" breathes Quentin. Then before your eyes, the lumpy, mushroomlike features reshape themselves and become human. Falling to his knees, Quentin grasps your hands and cries, "I will never forget this. My life and my allegiance are yours forever."

Your face turns red. "Please get up. I'm sure you'd do the same for me. What we need to do now is get out of here. Any ideas?"

There is a thoughtful silence. Then Owl asks, "How is the mushroom potion delivered to the magicians?"

Quentin's face lights up. "That's it! When a batch is ready, we release a homing bat with a note attached to its leg. Soon afterward, a messenger appears and collects the potion. Morel! Quick, fetch me a bat!" Turning to you, he adds, "Then, when the messenger arrives, we'll force him to show us the way out of here."

Morel stumps away and then returns holding a squeaking, struggling bat.

Quentin finds a scrap of paper, writes "Potion ready," and fastens it to the leg of the wriggling bat.

As the animal flutters away into the darkness, you notice the mushroom men doing something very odd. They are scraping the glowing silver fungus off the walls of the cavern and smearing it on their bodies.

"What are they doing?" you ask Fox.

"Looks like they're preparing for battle, you know, kind of like war paint."

"But why?"

"Us hate wizards," growls a mushroom man. "Not want to work for them. Sacred mushrooms belong to us. They plunder our fields. Soon mushrooms be gone and we have nothing but dirt. Then us starve. Us go too!"

1) If you agree to take the mushroom people with you, turn to page 17.

2) If you don't want to take them, turn to page 11.

"I'm glad we're staying here," you say. "Pentegarn might not find us if we leave."

"But I could guide us," says Owl. "There is nothing to be gained by staying here. We must not depend on others if we can help ourselves."

"Buzz off, Beak Breath," Fox says from the safety of your lap. "Jaimie says we stay, so I say so, too. If you don't like it, you can just fly away."

"No, Fox. I won't go. We're all in this together. I'll stay, too," says Owl as he settles down on a cloud beside you.

Time passes slowly. The drifting, misty, cottony clouds make you dreamy. You find that you have no wish to move, think, or act.

After a time, you notice that your body and that of Fox and Owl are becoming transparent. If you squint and look through Owl, you can see clouds passing behind him. You know you should be worried, but that's something humans do. And you're not human anymore — you're a cloud. So you close your eyes and drift away in the wind.

THE END

"Fox is right!" you exclaim. "The only way to deal with a dragon is with violence. It's the only thing a dragon understands!"

Ignoring Owl's pleas, you pull out your dagger and begin creeping toward the caves.

"Come on, Feather Face, or are you too chicken?" sneers Fox.

"No, Fox, I am not a 'chicken,' as you so cleverly put it," says Owl, and he joins you reluctantly. "I doubt the wisdom of this choice. But since we are comrades, I will not leave you now."

With dagger drawn, you approach the cave opening. At last you reach it and, sliding around the corner, you come eye to eye with the largest of the dragons. "Uh—um—excuse me," you stammer. "M-m-my friends and I are lost and—um—we were wondering—um—if you could help us find the way home." Frantically you try to hide your dagger, which suddenly feels very, very large.

The dragon continues to stare at you with large, sad eyes. Its gaze drops down to your dagger, then back up to your face.

"Oh—um—you're wondering about my dagger, I see. Well—um—er—one can never be too careful, can one? It's really a very little dagger, you know. It couldn't really hurt anything."

The dragon continues to stare sadly at you. Somehow you know it doesn't believe you. Suddenly the dragon inhales deeply, bends toward you, and blows. A strange wind, both warm and cool, blows around you. You close your eyes and wonder if you are dying.

When you open them, you see in horror that you are sitting astride an enormous rainbow that arches high into the sky. Far below you, the mist-covered cloud cave grows smaller and smaller and finally disappears completely as you, Fox, Owl, and the rainbow streak across the sky.

"Mama, where did they go?" asks the smallest dragon. "Why did you blow a rainbow? There wasn't any rain."

"I know, my dear," sighs the large dragon. "But that was a human being. Humans are often dangerous. They believe in fighting and violence just for fun. I really didn't have any choice. I had to get rid of it because it might have hurt us." The dragon sighs. "It's hard to believe that creatures like that can really enjoy our beautiful rainbows."

"But where did it go, Mama?" insists the littlest dragon.

"I don't know, dear," answers the dragon. "Somewhere over the rainbow. But don't you worry your pretty little head over it. Come here and I'll tell you the story of 'Goldilocks and the Three Dragons.' "

And purring happily, the little dragon settles down for her story.

THE END

"I suppose I could use my levitation spell. It's still the only one I can count on working every time," you say.

"Well, don't just stand there, do it!" whines Fox. "Those creepy crawlies are getting awfully close."

Closing your eyes, you concentrate as hard as you can and utter the magic words. A long tense moment passes and then a cheer goes up from the others.

"Hurray! You did it!" cries Fox.

"My congratulations," says Owl.

You look up and see the rug pressed tightly against the ceiling. Small but constant squirmings remind you that if you stop concentrating, down will come the rug, spiders, and all.

Keeping your eyes on the wriggling rug, you whisper, "We'd better decide what we're going to do from here—and quickly!"

"Our choices are obvious," says Owl.

1) "Open the door." Turn to page 41.

2) "We could climb out the window." Turn to page 12.

3) "Or see if there is a way to exit through the fireplace." Turn to page 105.

"Let's go this way. It smells kind of earthy. Maybe it's the way up," you say.

"Yeah, sure. And maybe I'm a cute little bunny rabbit," grumbles Fox.

"I see strange lights ahead," says Owl.

Now you, too, can see lights, shimmering and shining with a rainbowlike glow. Looking at one closely, you see that it seems to be a fungus growing on the tunnel wall.

As you go on, the stone floor of the tunnel turns to rich, loamy soil. The tunnel itself widens into a cavern. The flickering light is just bright enough to show another corridor on the far side of the cavern. You also notice swaying, moving shadows on the walls. You are not alone!

"There are other creatures alive in this place," whispers Owl. "Their shapes suggest that they are somewhat like humans."

"They smell funny, whatever they are," mutters Fox. "Sort of like moldy plants."

"We had best decide our actions," whispers Owl. "They're moving this way!"

1) "I'm not afraid of them," Fox barks bravely. "Let's fight them." If this is your choice, turn to page 37.

2) "Maybe we should try to talk to them," you say. If this is your choice, turn to page 58.

"EEEEowwwlll!" howls Fox in anguish.

"Fox! Fox! Come here! Come to me!" you call into the wispy fog. And soon a cold nose pushes into your hand, and a trembling body presses against your leg.

"Where are we and how do we get home?" quavers Fox.

"I fear we are somewhere on the Plane of Elemental Air," says Owl. "Far from home."

"EEEEowwwlll!" howls Fox.

"Fox, stop! I'll get us home somehow," you say with a confidence you do not feel.

You gather the quivering fox into your arms and stroke his head to comfort him.

"Owl, why don't you fly around? See what you can see, then come back and tell us."

Nodding wisely, Owl hurtles into the pink mist and disappears swiftly.

Nervously, you sit down on the cottony material, which sags but holds you.

It seems hours before you hear the flap of wings. You give a shrill whistle, and soon Owl descends out of the mist.

"Your guidance call was most welcome, Jaimie," says Owl. "Everything looks much the same from above."

"Be polite later, Egg Face. What did you see? Can we get out of here?" asks Fox.

"I am uncertain as to an exact method of escape. I saw only two items of interest—one, a tall cloud castle, and two, a series of thundercloud mountains. The mountains are so sheer as to defy climbing. But they have a number of large caves in them that may be inhabited."

You sigh deeply. "Well, I guess I can't expect a sign that says: 'This way home.' But now what are we going to do?"

1) "They'll bring us back sooner or later, no matter who wins. Let's stay here and wait." Turn to page 64.

2) "Let's go check out that cloud castle." Turn to page 47.

3) "Let's go look at the cloud mountains and find out what lives in those caves." Turn to page 84.

Clutching the ring, you close your eyes and say, "I wish Pentegarn were here and everything was all right."

You hear an ominous clanking and a squawk of fear from Owl.

"Oh, no, kid! Now you've done it!" screeches Fox.

Opening your eyes, you see the armor figures, full size once again, advancing on the three of you, weapons at the ready.

"That's just what I was afraid of," you gasp as the ring crumbles to dust. "It was only a three-wish ring."

As you cower in fear and watch the advance of the fearful creatures, you wish that this were not

THE END

It is tempting to enter the doorway, but the cord seems to send out warm, friendly feelings that urge you on. Hand over hand, you follow it into the darkness.

Soon you hear a soft, soothing hum and see a faint light in the distance.

Grasping your dagger, you hurry forward.

You turn a corner and stop abruptly. Before you, sitting cross-legged on the ground, is a tiny old man wearing only rags. Long white hair, a beard, and a mustache drape over his shoulders. As he sits, he sways back and forth in time to a tuneless melody that flows through his ancient lips.

On the ground in front of him is a pile of smoothly polished many-sided stones. Each stone is the size of a walnut, and each side is a different color. The strange old man moves the stones, constantly changing their patterns on the ground. A large prism hangs above him, casting a thin, faded rainbow.

Grasping your dagger firmly, you step under the arch of the rainbow.

The old man looks up and focuses his faded blue eyes on you. He stares at you, Fox, and Owl and then exclaims, "It's you! You're the Ones! You're here at last!"

"The ones? What ones?" you ask.

"Why, the Ones I've been waiting for, of course. The Ones who will come for the key," says the old man impatiently.

"Key? What key?" you ask, growing ever more confused.

"THE key!" hollers the old man. "This one." Opening a leather pouch hung round his neck on a thong, he pulls out a small key covered with rainbow-colored scales.

You sheathe your dagger and say, "I'm confused. Let's talk. Maybe we can figure this out."

Sitting cross-legged on the floor across from the old man and the shimmering stones, you introduce yourself and your friends.

"I am ... I am Nesbitt," says the old man in a faltering voice, as though unused to speaking. "I am the Keeper of the Key. I have been here for a long time, waiting."

"Waiting for what? For whom?" you ask.

"Why, for you, of course!" says the old man in surprise. "The Rainbow Dragons told me to wait until you came, a young human, an animal, and a bird. Others have tried to take it from me, but I have kept it safe."

"Rainbow Dragons? What are they and what is this the key to?" you ask in wonder.

"I ... I don't remember," says the old man, putting a hand to his head. "It was such a long time ago. But it's yours now." And opening the pouch, he hands you the key.

"Why don't you start from the beginning?" you say, staring at the key in puzzlement.

"When I first came here, King Chromos was dying and the kingdom was attacked by the forces of evil. The dragons gave me the key and told me to wait for you. I was afraid of the dark, so they gave me the cord to light my way and the stones to protect me. But I was too afraid to follow the cord and I've forgotten how to use the stones."

"What do the stones do?" asks Fox, sniffing at them suspiciously.

"They are my protection. Watch," says Nesbitt. With thin, birdlike fingers he arranges the stones in a circle around the four of you. Instantly a brilliant rainbow mist surrounds you. "Anyone trying to enter the circle will disappear," says Nesbitt. "The stones will do other things, too,"—he sighs—"but I've forgotten the patterns."

"Like what things can they do?" you ask.

"Like take you places, away from here. But I've been waiting so long that my thinker is a little rusty and I've forgotten how."

"Wouldn't you like to leave here? See trees and grass and the sky again?" you ask.

"Trees? Grass? Sky? I know those words," says Nesbitt excitedly. "At least I used to!"

"Well, it's clear we need to get out of here," you say. "The only question is how."

1) "I think we should keep following the cord," says Fox. "It probably leads outside." If this is your choice, turn to page 116.

2) "I think we should try to make the stones work," you say. If this is your choice, turn to page 92.

"I suggest we investigate this very interesting door in the wall," whispers Owl.

"Owl, for once I agree with you," barks Fox. "Let's get out of here."

The three of you slip through the wall into darkness. Once through, you press the stones, and the wall slides back into place.

"ooooooo!" cries the ghostly voice faintly from the other side of the wall.

"I don't know if it can get in here or not, but let's not hang around waiting to find out," says Fox as he rushes away.

Holding your hands in front of you, you walk through the darkness. Then, without warning, you bump into something that falls with the clatter of metal.

Quickly you drop to the ground and scurry away, but nothing happens.

A terrified shriek pierces the gloom.

"Fox! Fox! Are you all right? Answer me!"

Something bumps into you, and you quickly rise in fear.

"It's me, kid," says Fox in a whisper. "We're surrounded, but something's weird—they don't move and I can't smell them."

Just then, you are blinded by an intense light. Seconds later, Owl settles on your shoulder. "Where did the light come from?" you ask.

"I used basic logic. I pulled the tapestries back from the windows."

Blinking against the sudden light, you see figures—hundreds of them—clad in armor and holding assorted weapons. Small metal rainbow arches are attached to each armored breast. Arched shields are brilliant rainbow colors. The strange frozen figures stand silent, covered with dust, in the middle of the enormous room.

You move cautiously from one figure to the next, staring at them in awe. Silent and still, they tower above you, with metal hands clutching shields, swords, maces, battle axes, crossbows, and other weapons. Row after row of iron warriors stare at you. Hundreds of weapons hang on the rough stone walls. Rainbow-striped banners hang in tatters from the ceilings.

"It appears to be an armory, or perhaps a museum of sorts," says Owl. "Fear not. They cannot harm us. They are but shells of their former selves."

"Listen, kid, why don't you grab a weapon? I'd feel better if we had something solid to protect us."

"You know I can't do that! I may be only an apprentice magic user, but magic users aren't allowed to use large weapons."

"That's the dumbest thing I've ever heard," mutters Fox. "You only know those baby spells that backfire and do weird things to us as well as the enemy."

"Not always! Sometimes I get them right. I'm getting better all the time, and Pentegarn's promised that if I practice hard, he'll teach me some new spells real soon."

"But this is here and now. Isn't there something here you can use?"

Walking among the armored men, you notice a small figure wearing a cloth suit and a cloak and hood similar to one Pentegarn frequently wears, except this cloak is banded with bright stripes of rainbow colors.

On the first finger of the figure's glove is a peculiar ring covered with symbols that seem familiar. But what interests you most is that the gloved hands hold a thick wooden staff with forged iron covering each end.

"I could use this," you say, and reaching up, you try to pry it loose from the gloved hands. You pull the staff sideways, but the grip of the gloves is too tight. You pull down as hard as you can. There is a stiff jerk and the arms and staff move back to their original position.

"I must be imagining this!" you say angrily. You take a firm grip and pull down again. Again the staff moves upward, but it does not stop until it reaches the figure's shoulder.

"This is ridiculous!" you snort, and you pry the fingers up one by one. As you pull the staff free from one hand, the hand moves and clutches at air. As it does so, the ring slips off its finger and falls to the ground. Groping wildly, the hand finds its staff and grips it so firmly that you know you will never free it again. Your eye is caught by the fallen ring. You pick the ring up and look at it with curiosity.

"How did it move like that?" asks Fox.

"Don't worry," you whisper. "It's just gravity or something."

A rough, jagged screech of unoiled metal shatters the silence. As it echoes through the hall, you see an armored figure holding a two-handed broadsword step down from its pedestal. You stare in terror as it staggers unsteadily toward you, like a baby learning to walk.

"Oh, my gosh! If that's gravity, I'm a wolf. Let's get out of here, kid!"

But before you can even move, you hear a peculiar rhythmic swishing noise. Turning, you almost faint with fright.

Standing on a raised platform on your left is a huge figure covered from head to toe with chain mail and metal plates. One upraised hand clutches a short rod of iron. Attached to the rod is a stout chain ending in a large spiked metal ball. Around and around the metal man's head the ball swishes through the air. Faster and faster it goes until the air whistles with its passage. Then the creature moves toward you.

"May I suggest that we abandon these premises with much haste," chirps Owl.

You turn to flee . . . but yet another suit of armor begins to stir. Its helmet is shaped like a ram's head, with cruelly pointed, curling horns. It swivels in your direction. A blank, black space filled with evil stares at you from narrow eye slits.

Spiked gloves glisten as metal hands tighten around the handle of the battle axe. The iron

monster takes a step toward you as it heaves the axe to its shoulder.

"Every man for himself!" barks Fox. Seconds later you hear a terrible twang and a fox howl that ends abruptly.

Turning, you see an arrow buried in the floor. Fox dangles upside down, blood dripping from his head, gripped by the metal fist of an armored archer.

Clenching your fists in fear and anger, your fingers close upon the ring that the cloaked figure dropped. Almost unconsciously, you slip it on your finger.

You hear all around you the sounds of metal figures stirring, as if waking from a long sleep, and coming closer and closer.

"Jaimie, we must take some action or our opportunities for action will be ended," insists Owl.

1) "Maybe we should just run away." If this is your choice, turn to page 35.

2) "Maybe they're not really so bad. We could try to talk to them." Turn to page 122.

3) "A trick! I wish we could think of a trick that would work." Turn to page 145.

"I'm not sure that ignoring a problem will make it go away," says Pentegarn, sighing. "But we can try it and see if it works."

Five days later, on a beautiful summer morning, as you work on your wizardry lessons, snow suddenly begins to fall. By noon it covers the castle's doors, and by evening it reaches the upper walls. A freezing wind blows, and icicles hang from the ceilings in every room. Owl's beak is frozen shut and Fox shivers in the ashes in the fireplace, where a fire refuses to burn.

"I think maybe I should change my mind," you say, breathing through a reddened nose.

"Agreed," says Pentegarn. "When do we leave?"

"In the morning," you reply between sneezes, and you hurry away to find another coat.

Please turn to page 110.

Walking on the pink fluff toward the thundercloud mountains is very difficult. The stuff pulls at your legs like quicksand. Every step is an effort. In a short time, you and Fox are exhausted. Yet the cloud mountains still seem far away.

"Not another step!" declares Fox.

"It's unfortunate that I cannot share the gift of wings," says Owl, flapping easily above you. "There is quite a pleasant wind blowing."

Suddenly an idea strikes you!

"Owl, come down here. I have a great idea." Quickly you take off your long billowing cape. "Now, I want you to take the top of this cape in your claws and I'll hold onto the bottom, close my eyes, and concentrate on levitating. Fox can climb into my vest. The way I figure it, when I get up high enough, the wind will catch the cloak like a sail and blow us over to the mountains! What do you think? Isn't that a good idea?"

"Ask me in an hour," mutters Fox.

"Truly an inspired concept," says Owl as he gathers up the cloak in his claws.

You close your eyes, concentrate, hang on to the cloak and . . . up, up, up you go. The wind grabs hold of the material, fills it full, and instantly you are flying through the misty air at a fast pace. But suddenly the wind shifts and, before you can adjust the cloak, you are turning head over heels in the air.

"Help!" barks Fox.

You open your eyes in confusion and—zip!—the three of you plunge downward until you stop abruptly somewhere in midcloud.

"You know the one nice thing about flying here?" asks Fox as he climbs up out of a deep, puffy cloud hole. "When you crash, it doesn't hurt!"

Although you take a few more falls, you soon master the method and are soaring easily through the sky.

"The cloud caves are visible," says Owl. "I estimate our arrival time to be three minutes. I recommend we make an indirect approach. I cannot see the residents of the caves, but it never hurts to be cautious."

1) If you want to ignore Owl's advice and land directly in front of the caves, turn to page 90.

2) If you want to follow Owl's advice and land under the cloud cover in front of the caves, turn to page 44.

"Obviously you do not know about the peculiar appetite of rust monsters," says Owl.

"Owl, no lectures! Not now! Let me clear this monster out of the way first, then you can talk all you want!"

"Oh, the impatience of youth," sighs the bird.

"Oh, dear. Oh, dear," moans the old man.

"Come on, Jaimie. I'm with you, kid," says Fox. "Don't let these fuddy-duddies get you down."

You move your dagger, and quickly—so quickly that you are later unsure that you really saw it—the rust monster lifts its long snout and spits a fine mist at your dagger. Before your astonished eyes, your weapon rusts and crumbles into a fine powder, which falls to the ground.

The rust monster snuffles joyfully, and waddles up to the powder. A long tongue slurps out and laps up every crumb of rust. Lifting its long snout, the monster looks at you with dim, watery, gray eyes, as though checking you for more metal. Then snuffling happily, the strange creature waddles off into the darkness.

"Did you see that!" you exclaim, looking at your empty hand.

"I did try to alert you to the unusual dietary habits of the creature," says Owl.

"Maybe if you'd talk English instead of Dictionary, we'd be able to understand you," snarls Fox.

"Really, Fox! Your grasp of decent vocabulary is abysmal," sniffs Owl, ruffling his feathers.

"We can argue later," you say. "What do we do now?

1) "We could go down this other passage here on my left. It seems kind of foolish to go in the dark and without weapons, but going back doesn't make much sense either. Maybe we can find the way out." If this is your choice, turn to page 23.

2) "Perhaps we should try to use Nesbitt's stones to get out of here." Turn to page 92.

"I don't like her," snaps Fox. "She's rude, nasty, and loud. I say leave her here."

"I agree with my furry colleague," says Owl. "The princess would find our activities entirely unsatisfactory and disrupt the party. I, too, vote to leave her."

You glance fearfully at Imogene, whose face is turning a deep, dark red.

"I'm sorry, Imogene," you say nervously. "I really wouldn't have minded a whole lot if you had come. But the majority rules. So I guess we'll be going now. It's been real nice meeting you. I hope everything works out all right for you. Take care of yourself," you add, gulping, as you edge toward the door.

THUD! The heavy door slams shut behind you. Click! It locks itself.

"HA! If I can't leave, neither can you!" shouts Imogene gleefully.

"What? Let me out!" hollers Fox.

"Calm yourself, Fox," says Owl. "Jaimie will unlock the door and we'll leave. Jaimie, please use the key."

"Key? I thought you had it. Fox?"

"Key? Quit kidding. You know I don't have it. Now open that door! I couldn't stand it if we were truly trapped with this kid."

You open your empty hands and stare in horror at your friends.

Imogene smiles smugly, then opens her mouth and begins to scream.

THE END

You land in front of the caves with a gentle bump. Their openings rise high above you and pulse with a curious multicolored glow. Puzzled, you take a few cautious steps into the largest cave. On the floor before you are heaps and mounds of bright, shining color—red, blue, green, yellow, violet, and so on—all the colors of the rainbow. Against the wall of the cave are three large nests, built out of the cottony-soft cloud material.

Astonished, you walk farther into the cave and look at the piles of color.

"What can this be?" you ask.

"I don't know and I don't want to find out," whines Fox. "Look at the size of those nests. Whatever lives here is too big for me. I'm getting out!"

You turn to argue, but the words die on your lips and you stand in silent terror.

Crowding into the mouth of the cave are three dragons, and they are all glaring at you.

"Intruders!" squeaks the smallest dragon.

"Robbers!" growls the medium dragon.

"LUNCH!" roars the largest dragon.

You back up slowly, excuses coming to your lips and dying unsaid. You know you are not really an intruder. You're not a robber. And you hope with all your heart that you're not lunch.

THE END

"Let's leave. I don't like them and I think they would cheat. They'd find some way of tricking us. I think we should go to the Council, tell them what's happened, and ask them to give you back your rights."

"Gentlemen," says Pentegarn, turning back to the wizards, "my colleague and I have conferred and decided to withdraw."

Under the scornful eyes of the wizards, the four of you leave Rainbow Castle.

Long months later you enter the chambers of the Grand Council.

"Pentegarn, Jaimie, Fox, and Owl, I am glad to see you safe. I have followed your adventures with a heavy heart and yearned to help," says the Great Grand Wizard, "but one must not disturb the balance. It is not allowed. And so, even though your cause is just, I cannot help. Your district was fairly claimed by Malus, Pothos, and Rubus. Now, you must either meet their challenge and win, or leave the Pillars forever."

"OK," you say. "We've tried this and it didn't work, so let's go back and show those three what magic is all about!"

"Well said, Jaimie!" says Pentegarn.

"Can I bite one of them?" asks Fox.

"Typical response from one of your mentality," snipes Owl.

"Good luck," says the Great Grand Wizard as you turn back to Rainbow Castle.

Please turn to page 133.

"May I see the stones, Nesbitt?" you ask gently. "Maybe new eyes will be able to unravel their secret."

Reluctantly, Nesbitt hands them to you.

Holding them up to the faint light of the broken cord, you notice that each stone has a different color on each of its many sides.

"What do you make of this, Owl?"

"It appears to be a code," answers Owl. "Perhaps if the colors were matched up to each other, their meaning would become clear."

"Colors? What colors?" asks Nesbitt, pushing his face close to the stones. "I can't see them. Long ago there used to be colors, but they disappeared."

"No, Nesbitt," you say kindly. "The colors are here. Living so long in the dark has probably hurt your vision.

"Perhaps you're right, Owl. If we match the colors that are the same . . . hmmmmm."

You try many different combinations, but nothing happens. You study the stones, hoping to discover what their maker might have meant. You empty your mind and drift, becoming one with the stones. Blankness. Thickness. Images of rainbow colors. Understanding. Coming back. Being Jaimie.

"I understand," you say quietly. And picking up the stones, you fit them together in a way that you know is right.

"Quickly, gather together!" you tell everyone as the stones cast a circle of brilliant color and begin to hum. Pressing close together,

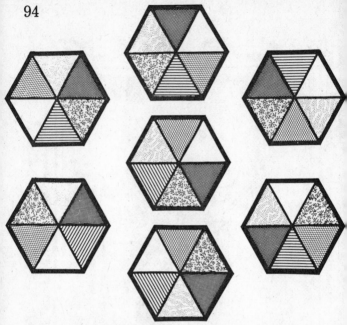

Can you make the stones work?
Cut out or trace these stones. Pick one stone to go in the middle and arrange the rest around it so that all touching edges match.

your group kneels around the shining circle of stones.

A strange feeling comes over you—tingling, whispery. Looking down, you give a sharp cry. Your feet and legs are gone! Most of Fox and Owl are gone! Alarmed, you tug at your hand, held firmly by Nesbitt.

"Do not break the connection," warns the old man. "We're going back! Trust the stones. They will not harm you."

The nothingness creeps farther up your body. You close your eyes and try to trust.

And then, there is a time of whirling nothingness, a rainbow arch, and a terrible sense of tearing.

"Where are we?" you ask, pressing your hands to your aching head.

"Oh, oh! Don't look now, but we're back," warns Fox.

Opening your eyes, you look straight into the angry eyes of Malus.

"Where did you come from?" he asks angrily, poking you with a knobby finger. "And who's this hairy old man?"

"His name's Nesbitt. I found him in your wonderful game room. He says the Rainbow Dragons told him to wait there for me, and he gave me this." You hold up the key. It glows and pulses in your hand.

"It's THE KEY!" whispers Malus, his eyes wide. Then he calms himself and says, "I see you have found our key. Heh, heh, heh. It was really a test. We sent you to the game room to see if you could find it for us. You passed the test. You can give it to me now."

"Don't trust him, kid!" whispers Fox.

"Where is Pentegarn?" chirps Owl.

"Is this outside? I remember it being brighter," says Nesbitt.

"Where's Pentegarn?" you demand, holding the key behind your back.

"Don't worry about him—he's finished! Just give us the key," demands Rubus.

Suddenly, you notice that all three wizards hold magical amulets in their hands.

"You cheated!" you shout. "You said no magical devices were allowed. Where's Pentegarn? What have you done with him?"

"Give us the key and we'll give you your precious Pentegarn," snarls Malus.

"Here's your old key. I don't want it!" you cry, throwing the key across the room. All three wizards throw themselves upon it.

"Mine!" cries Pothos. "I saw it first!"

"Mine! I'm oldest!" screams Rubus.

"It's mine! I'm the best!" hollers Malus.

As you watch, all three wizards grasp the key at the same time. Instantly, there is a deafening noise and a bright flash, and you are thrown to the floor.

Picking yourself up, you look for the wizards and the key. You see the sparkling key on the floor. Next to it sits a large fat toad, eyes bulging with alarm. A long, slender black snake is draped over the toad's head. At that moment, the toad and the snake spot an ugly furry black spider crawling across the floor. There is a frantic hopping and slithering as both creatures chase the spider through the open doors and out of your sight.

Confused and frightened, you hurry to Pentegarn's side. "Pentegarn, wake up!"

"I'm not dead yet, Jaimie. You don't have to shout! But I have felt better." Staggering to his feet, the old wizard tries to focus his eyes. "Where are they? They tricked me!"

"Don't worry, Pentegarn. They're gone. I think they were changed into a toad, a snake, and a spider." Turning, you pick up the key. "This had something to do with it."

"Drop it!" Pentegarn cries, slapping frantically at your hand.

"It's all right," you say. "I've held it before and nothing happened to me. I got it from Nesbitt here, who says that a bunch of dragons told him a long time ago to give it to me. Isn't that right, Nesbitt?"

"What? What? Yes, that's right. Cobalt, King of the Rainbow Dragons, gave it to me. He said that when you came you would know how to use it."

"It's the Key to the Kingdom, Jaimie," says Pentegarn with awe in his voice.

"Once, long ago, the kingdom was united under King Chromos and the Rainbow Dragons. Life was more beautiful than you could ever imagine.

"But the keepers grew old and they knew that an heir must be found, someone worthy to carry on in place of Chromos. The test they devised was simple. You had to pick up the key and hold it . . . if you could. Many tried. Those who were evil and unworthy were changed forever to that which they most resembled in life. If you were good but not worthy, you received a powerful shock. I was one of those, and I still bear the scar.

"Before Chromos died, he decided that no one yet alive was worthy to hold the key."

"And then Cobalt gave the key to me," interrupts Nesbitt. "And told me to wait until you came for it. Those Rainbow Dragons who were left in the castle came out and flew away. The sky glowed with their colors and then they were gone and everything turned gray."

"Once they were gone, evil entered the land," continues Pentegarn.

"But what does it mean?" you ask, looking at the rainbow-colored key.

"It means that you are the ruler of the land now," explains Nesbitt patiently. "Whoever holds the Key to the Kingdom is the king. Evil will flee before you, and goodness will return to the land. And best of all, the dragons will come back.

"That's enough jabbering. Isn't there something called food?" grumbles Nesbitt. "As your first act as ruler of the Rainbow Kingdom, how about bringing me some?" But before you can reply, a wondrous thing happens. The ugly gray walls seem to quiver and slowly begin to change colors. First beige, then cream, then yellow, orange, red, green, blue, purple—all the joyous colors of the spectrum—until they become a glorious shimmer of every happy color in the world.

As you stare in wonder, the sound of wings beating the air fills your ears. Looking upward in excitement, you see the first of the Rainbow Dragons coming home.

THE END

"I'd really like to be powerful," you say, sorely tempted. "And I'd like to be wise. But getting back and seeing if Pentegarn needs to be rescued is the most important."

Placing your finger on the page, you begin working your way through the difficult spell.

At last you reach the final word. Pausing before you speak, you look around you at the wonderful room. Books—delightful books you wish you had time to read—still spill out of cases. The tapestry seems so alive that you could almost step into it and disappear. Fox still lies curled on the dictionary, with a smile on his face.

You smile sadly to yourself and hope that whatever happens, Fox and Owl will be all right, free to continue their never-ending battle. Then you utter the last magic word.

Head over heels, you tumble through a dark and weightless void and land sprawling on the cold stones of the Great Hall of the Rainbow Castle. Inches from your face lies an unmoving Pentegarn. Scrambling to his side, you shake him gently and call his name. A low moan escapes his lips, but Pentegarn does not waken.

"It's the brat!" hisses an evil voice.

Turning, you look up into the faces of the three wizards. Each holds a magical device.

"You said no magic items were allowed," you exclaim, enraged.

Instantly, the devices disappear from the hands of the wizards.

"You can't prove it! We'll deny it! It will be your word against ours!" screeches Malus.

"Never mind about the brat! Look what came with it!" hisses Rubus.

"It's the BOOK!" gasps Pothos. And all three wizards dive for the book from the library, which lies at your feet.

"Quick! Open it! Here, let me do it, you clumsy fool!" yells Malus.

Snapping it open impatiently, he turns page after page. Ignoring the wizards, you try to revive Pentegarn.

"It's empty! All the spells are gone!" shrieks Malus. "The brat has erased them!"

"It's a trick!" hisses Rubus as he grabs you by the neck and pulls you to your feet.

Placing his cruel face next to yours, he hisses, "If you ever hope to see Pentegarn alive again, make those words reappear."

Too afraid to admit you know nothing, you take the heavy book in your trembling hands, and it opens beneath your fingers.

A golden glow shimmers in the left-hand corner of the page and then turns into tiny gold letters.

The wizards gasp in shock as the little letters sort themselves out, dance over the page, and arrange themselves in neat lines. "How to Be Powerful," reads one. "How to Be Wise," reads another.

"That's for me!" says Malus. And pushing you away, he reads the second spell aloud. There is a whirling of wind, a dulling of time, and then he is gone, vanished from the face of the earth, and so is the spell.

Now only one spell remains on the page. Screaming and pushing, Rubus and Pothos shove each other in their struggle to reach the book first. Almost in the same breath, they read the spell aloud.

A mighty crack of thunder crashes through the hall and then they are gone. Gone too are the gold letters on the page.

In the sudden silence you hear Fox moan, "This is all your fault."

"I fail to understand your reasoning or lack of it, as the case may be," groans Owl.

"I'm sure it's your fault. I couldn't have gotten a headache like this on my own. If you hadn't forced me to drink that stuff, I'd be OK. I'm going to lie down for a while," says Fox as he staggers over to Pentegarn, lies down on a corner of his robe, and goes to sleep.

"Too much noise," says Owl as Fox begins to snore, and he flaps up to a rafter, closes his eyes, and tucks his head beneath a wing.

Putting the book down on the floor, you kneel at Pentegarn's side and watch anxiously. After a while, his eyes flutter open and focus on you.

"Jaimie, what's happened? Where are the wizards? They tricked me. They used hidden magical amulets." Groaning and using your shoulder for support, he rises shakily.

"EARTHQUAKE!" screams Fox as he slides onto the cold floor.

"It's all right. They're gone and I don't think we'll ever see them again," you say.

"How can you be so sure, Jaimie?" asks Pentegarn wearily.

"Well, it's this book," you say, picking it up from the floor. "They got real excited when they saw it. But it wouldn't work for them. For some reason, it worked for me, but as soon as they used the spells, they disappeared and so did the spells. Now it's all empty." You thumb through the pages to show him. But to your astonishment, as you turn the pages, you see the golden glow of letters lurking in the corner of each page.

Stunned, you hold one page open and instantly the fat little letters swarm over the page and line themselves up obediently, waiting to be read.

"I don't understand," you say in a whisper. "They were all gone. All the pages were empty. Now they're back, hundreds of them— and I can't even understand one word."

Placing his hands on your shoulders, Pentegarn looks into your eyes and says, "Jaimie, you have been given a great gift, a great honor. Someone, some presence, saw fit to aid you. This book contains all the spells that King Chromos gathered during his long lifetime. You cannot expect to understand all that he knew in one brief glance. I suspect that even if you study hard, it will take all of your lifetime to learn the wisdom contained in this book. A worthy goal, child, and a great honor.

"But first, we must clean the cobwebs of evil from this castle and try to undo all that those three did during their stay here. I will need your help. I cannot do it all by myself. And if we are very, very fortunate, perhaps the Rainbow Dragons will return to this, their ancestral home."

Smiling happily, you look around the Great Hall, which no longer seems so ominous.

Scooping Fox up off the stones, you hug him to your chest.

"Avalanche," murmurs Fox, burying his nose in his tail.

Safe and happy, you follow Pentegarn, ready to face anything that Rainbow Castle has to offer.

THE END

"I don't want to climb down this tower!" whines Fox.

"Neither do I. I don't like high places," you say. "Let's try the fireplace."

Still concentrating on keeping the spiders trapped at the ceiling, you edge backward into the fireplace.

"It sure is dark in here," you say, groping about in total darkness.

"It usually is inside fireplaces," snaps Fox. "Where to now, Pathfinder?"

"Down," says Owl. "I perceive a staircase to our left. I know not where it leads, but it seems unlikely that we will encounter the wizards here. So let us proceed."

Holding Fox in your arms, you start down the dark narrow stairway. All of a sudden, the stairs disappear beneath your feet and you begin to slide. Faster and faster you move. WHOMP! You crash into Owl, who collapses into your lap. Rushing along at a fearful speed, you try to grip the walls and brace yourself against the downward plunge, but you cannot.

"I seem to have made a mistaaaaaaake!" screeches Owl.

There is a sense of weightlessness, of flying through the air. And then you abruptly crash to a stop. All is silent except for a muttered moan.

Please turn to page 33.

"Here it is—it's the last one," says Quentin, handing you a little brown furry creature.

As it chirps and twitters in your hands, Owl peers down from your shoulder and says, "Hmm, I fear this is an unwise course of action. Perhaps I should just eat the creature and take it off your hands."

"EEEPP!" screeches the bat.

"Owl, behave yourself," you say sternly. "We need its help."

"Ahem, excuse me," says Owl. "A brief lapse. I don't know what came over me."

Quickly you unravel the edge of your tunic and tie a thread to the leg of the bat. As Owl glares hungrily, the bat squeaks and flies off into the tunnel. The string rips through your fingers. "Let's go! It's working!" you cry, rushing into the dark tunnel.

Your way is lit by the glow of the shuffling mushroom men as you follow the bat through the corridors. You wonder if the bat really knows the way, but spurred on by its fear of Owl, it flaps steadily along.

"I don't think Ding Bat up there knows his nose from his toes," says Fox.

"Give it a chance. It's going somewhere."

"The alternatives please me," smirks Owl. "If it knows the path, we escape the dungeon. If it fails, I shall have a pleasant snack."

At long last, you round a corner and see a glimmer of light far ahead.

"How do you think we should do this?" you ask. "I mean, do we just walk right in? Maybe we should talk about this and make a plan."

"No talk," say the mushroom men. Brushing you aside, they stomp forward in a solid mass. Throwing open a set of large doors, they stride into the Great Hall. Loud cries erupt from the room.

Hurrying to the doorway, you see an amazing sight. The mushroom men surround Malus, Pothos, and Rubus, who cower in fear. Then Malus points a silver object, and one of the mushroom men falls to the floor.

Rubus strikes a mushroom on the shoulder, and it dissolves in a puddle of mush.

Pothos screams unknown words, and three more mushroom men freeze in their tracks.

But no matter what the wizards do, as soon as one mushroom man falls, two others take its place, pushing and crowding the wizards closer and closer together.

"Help!" scream the wizards, as their magic items are wrenched from their hands and crushed beneath the feet of the mushroom men.

"I'm afraid we'd better stop them before they kill those three," you say. "Killing them is no answer."

"True," Quentin agrees grimly, and the two of you wade into the fray.

"We'll do anything you say, give you anything you want! Just don't let those things hurt us!" cry the wizards.

"Where's Pentegarn?" you demand.

"Where's Imogene?" snarls Quentin.

"Pentegarn's over there. He's not hurt, just a little bent. Princess Imogene is all right, too. She's tucked away in her play castle. We'll bring her back immediately."

"Fix friends," the mushroom men say as they point to their fallen comrades.

"Of course! Our pleasure!" cries Malus. He makes several magical gestures. And to your amazement, all of the fallen mushroom men rise, seemingly unharmed.

As Malus is led away to revive Pentegarn, Quentin says, "Well, that takes care of almost everything. Once Pentegarn and Imogene are restored to us, we'll still have to undo all the mischief they did around here. But I'm sure that the three of us can do it and rule this land wisely."

"What shall we do with your uncles?" you ask. "We can't let them wander around creating trouble left and right."

"Turn them into plump rabbits," drools Fox.

"No, turn them into juicy field mice," says Owl, eyes gleaming.

"No, I think we should turn them over to the mushroom men and let them plant and tend mushrooms until they truly repent. That's what we should do," you say. And from the circle of smiles, you know you have made the right decision.

THE END

It is snowing as you and your friends set off for Rainbow Castle. "It seems as though our opponents are able to sway the seasons," observes Owl, as trees, rocks, and hills disappear in the whiteness.

"Yeah, and this snow is no fun either," says Fox, plunging through nose-deep snow.

"You could have stayed at home, Fox. You didn't have to come."

"Oh, no. If something horrible happens, I'd rather know about it right away. And besides, you guys need me."

Swallowing your laughter, you turn to Pentegarn. "Sir, why don't you do something about this snow? Why don't you perform some magic and change it back to summer?"

"Think, Jaimie. If our foes are putting all their efforts into creating winter just to annoy us, they can't send anything really dangerous against us. And they will believe that they have us in their power."

You wipe your cold, dripping nose and try to appreciate Pentegarn's plan, but the snow melts inside your boots, slithers down your neck, and freezes on your eyelashes. Even Pentegarn is sniffling by the time Rainbow Castle comes into view several days later.

"Why do they call it Rainbow Castle?" you ask, staring at the cascades of dirty gray ice that drape over the black towers and hang from the narrow, barred windows. A cold, bitter wind wails around the grim walls and plucks and tears at your clothes.

"In my youth, it was a beautiful place," Pentegarn answers sadly.

"It looks like it's all closed for the winter. How about we go home and wait for spring?" whines Fox.

"Ah, spring! Good idea!" says Pentegarn. "Rainbow Castle is beautiful in the spring!" And with a snap of his fingers, snow and ice begin to melt. Inch by inch, foot by foot, winter retreats, and in its place—warm, soft and green—spring comes to the land. Birds sing, flowers bloom, and gentle breezes blow. But the castle remains gray and gloomy.

"That's much better. And now they know we're here," says Pentegarn.

"Ah, Sweet Spring, full of sweet days and roses," sighs Owl, spreading his great wings to the sun.

"Why can't you speak plain English, Mouse Breath?" snarls Fox.

"I was just noting the welcome arrival of this magical spring, O Illiterate One."

"What did you call me?" barks Fox.

"Fox! Owl! Stop this bickering now, or I'll send you both home," you say firmly.

Fixing the two with a stern gaze, you quickly get out of your winter clothes and hurry after Pentegarn.

"And here are our hosts," says Pentegarn.

Three men stand at the end of the bridge. One is tall and thin, one is very, very fat, and the third is as tiny as a small child.

"See here, Pentegarn, what is the meaning

of this?" demands the tall, thin wizard. "An outrage I say! This warm weather will not be tolerated! We prefer winter!" And with a wave of his hand and a loud clap of thunder, spring vanishes as if it had never been, and winter descends in a flurry of flakes.

"Tchh, tchh," clucks Pentegarn. "I was enjoying the spring myself," and with a gesture and a sheet of lightning, winter is again replaced by spring.

The three wizards grind their teeth in rage, their faces purple with fury.

Now the tall wizard steps forward and begins to make magical gestures. Pentegarn replies with movements of his own. Sparks fly and sheets of flame erupt from the wizards, and winter and spring flicker in and out. The two wizards stand firm as the air crackles from white to blue, warm to cold.

At last, Pentegarn laughs a great booming laugh and slaps his knee. "Well done, Malus! But come, let's not confuse the birds any longer. Let it remain spring. Now that you've gotten us here, why don't you tell me what this is all about." Still laughing, he walks over and puts his arm around the unsmiling wizard's shoulders and begins to walk toward the castle.

As you follow Pentegarn into the castle, the high walls seem to swallow you up. Your footsteps echo hollowly as you enter a large room with three thronelike chairs set upon a raised platform. The wizards bump and push as they climb onto the platform, each trying to claim the center chair.

There are no other seats and you look about in discomfort as the wizards stare down at you with small, nasty smiles.

Pentegarn says, "Well, I see we need a few more chairs," and with a snap! two big, deep chairs of gold, studded with precious gems and covered with soft deep-purple velvet, appear behind you. Fox settles himself in a velvet-covered basket and Owl clings to a golden bird perch.

"Ah, that's better," says Pentegarn, sinking into his chair. Crossing his legs and folding his hands, he says, "Now then, gentlemen, what can we do for you?"

The wizards twitch nervously, pull their scraggly beards, and whisper. They seem to be urging each other to do something. Finally, tiny Rubus is levitated from his chair by one of his brothers. Stumbling to his feet, he draws himself to his full puny height, puffs up his chest, and says, "Pentegarn, you have been brought here to answer charges of practicing wizardry without a license. This area belongs to us. When you left, we applied to the Grand Council and they granted us control."

"How nice for you all," drawls Pentegarn. "I won't bother to ask why you never helped me in all the years I fought to rid the country of the Evil One, who caused me to 'leave,' as you put it. But I might ask why you never chased away the Evil One when he was certainly practicing a most unpleasant form of magic. I don't believe the council ever issued him a license."

"Ahh, umm, well, we just hadn't gotten around to it," squeaks Pothos from out of his great bulk. "Besides, he ate the first three messengers we sent."

"Indeed," says Pentegarn with a smile.

"But we are not the issue!" yells Pothos. "You are! You and your illegal apprentice. By order of the Grand Council, you and your brat and your zoo are under house arrest. You have two choices. Either leave and never again practice magic, under penalty of death! Or else meet us in a duel of skills."

"Allow me to confer with my apprentice," says Pentegarn, drawing you to his side.

"Well, Jaimie, what do you think we should do? These fellows appear very foolish and harmless, but that is not true. They are dangerous, and the council has given them the right to practice within this district. They are well within their rights to demand that we either quit or fight them. It is your decision as well as mine."

1) If you choose to challenge the wizards, turn to page 133.

2) If you choose to go to the Grand Council and argue, turn to page 91.

"If Nesbitt can't make the stones work for him, we probably won't be able to either," you say. "Fox is probably right. Let's follow the cord and try to find a way out."

"Take me with you, please," quavers the old man.

Helping him to his feet, you take hold of the rainbow-colored cord and start off down the dark corridor.

"Wait!" quavers the old man. And on shaky legs, he scurries back to his ruins, picks up the stones, and places them in his pouch. "I can't leave the stones for the monsters to find."

Once again you start down the corridor. Although you hear scary wailing and distant roars, no harm befalls you.

Suddenly you turn a corner, and the cord goes limp in your hand. There is no longer a line of light ahead of you. You reach out into the darkness and feel enormous boulders. A rock fall has broken the cord and blocked the corridor!

"We'll never be able to move these rocks," you say after climbing carefully to the top of the jumbled heap. "What do we do now?"

"I feel the presence of another passage directly to our right," says Owl. "Unfortunately, I also hear something approaching along that same passage."

Listening carefully, you hear the scraping of claws on rock. You draw your dagger and stare into the gloom, trying to see what is coming. Slowly a creature creeps into the dim light and stops, waving two long antennae in your direction.

"What is it?" you ask fearfully, clutching your dagger firmly.

"Armored, segmented carapace, long snout, large grinding molars, huge sharp claws," observes Owl. "It is quite obviously a rust monster. "I suggest we withdraw quickly and attempt to use the stones to project ourselves out of this dungeon."

1) If you choose to follow Owl's advice and withdraw, turn to page 92.

2) "It doesn't look too dangerous. I could just kill it and we could continue," you say. If this is your choice, turn to page 86.

"Look! We are not going to eat or drink anything unless we know where it comes from. It's too easy to slip poisons and potions into food and drink. As long as I'm in charge, I say no eating or drinking."

"Look, kid, I hate to remind you," says Fox patiently, "but it's thanks to you that we're here at all. And as far as being in charge goes, I vote we make it a democracy. Let's vote from now on. I'll feel safer."

"Okay. I vote for not eating or drinking. And I vote for exploring the castle to find out what that horrible noise is," you say.

"I second Jaimie's motion," chirps Owl.

"All right, all right. I lose this time, but I won't always," says Fox.

Passing the tempting table, the three of you agree to spread out to explore the castle for a short time, then gather to report your discoveries.

You let yourself be drawn toward the noise, and it grows louder and louder as you approach a staircase at the end of the hall. You stop there, however, and then double back to meet the others.

"There's nothing to be seen except a few broken windows and dents in the walls," reports Owl.

"All I found were lots of broken toys on the floor," says Fox in disgust, spitting out a headless doll.

"Odd, very odd," you say thoughtfully. "Well, I think I found where the noise is coming from—a staircase at the end of the hall. It doesn't sound like it's going to stop," you add, listening to the loud screeching. "Let's go find out what it is."

"And then push it out a window," grumbles Fox.

The three of you climb the steep winding stairway, your feet hesitating as the horrible noise grows louder as you climb.

The stairway ends abruptly in a single door. Although it seems thick and sturdy, it shakes under repeated heavy blows from the other side. The high, thin, horrible scream goes on and on. High on the wall above the door hangs a gold key.

You eye the key unhappily.

"Vote time!" screams Fox over the screeching. "I say let's get out of here. If someone went to all the trouble to build this castle and lock up whatever is making that horrible noise, I think we'd be real dumb to let it out!"

1) "Maybe it's just a protection device," says Owl. "Maybe there's a great treasure in there. Maybe the noise is a harmless illusion." If you want to find out what's behind the door, turn to page 19.

2) If you want to ignore the noise, leave the castle, and check out the caves, turn to page 84.

"Being powerful would be great! No one could hurt me. I wouldn't have to study ever again! And I could rescue Pentegarn."

Slowly, you pronounce the magic words. Then there is a terrible crash and a sense of change.

When the darkness clears from your eyes and mind, you look around with curiosity. A hand—a large powerful hand—moves in front of your face and smoothes back your hair. With a terrible sense of shock, you realize that it is YOUR hand. Fearfully, you look at the rest of your body. Powerful, gigantic muscles ripple beneath your skin. Thighs and legs the size of small trees support your massive body. Powerful muscles bulge with every breath. Even your hair feels tough!

Sitting at your huge feet are Fox and Owl, looking at you with awe and fear.

"Let's get out of here, Owl," whispers Fox, "before this giant stomps us flat!"

"Affirmative," answers Owl, and they rush out of the room into the world beyond.

Your powerful hearing has heard the whispered conversation and you lean out the window and shout, "Come back! It's me, Jaimie!" Your voice is a powerful bellow, and two small trees are blown over by its force. But the two animals disappear from sight.

As you stare down at yourself, you realize that you have made the wrong choice.

THE END

"Perhaps talking with them is not the wisest course of action, Jaimie," says Owl.

"What else can we do? We're surrounded. Where could we run to? I can't do any magic—there's too many of them. Pentegarn always says to use my brain and try to use reason before violence. Let's just hope these metal monsters are reasonable."

The first of the metal men are within striking distance. Screwing up your courage, you advance boldly and say, "Halt! We come in peace. We mean harm to no man."

But the creatures do not halt. They continue marching toward you, one clanking foot after another.

"Stop! Please stop! Can't we be friends?"

Clank! Clank! On they come. Retreating, you collide with a harsh, cold surface. Looking up, you peer into the black empty eye slits of the ram's-head helmet.

THE END

"I don't understand why I'm smelling this hot smell," mutters Fox.

Turning a corner, you stumble over a slab of rock heaped high with mushrooms.

"Wow! What is this place?" you exclaim.

Vaulted ceilings disappear in a tangle of stalactites that light the room with a soft green glow. And silvery veins of light streak the walls of the cave. Black glittering sand crunches underfoot.

"Look at this! " barks Fox in alarm.

Hurrying to his side, you stare down at the prints of two enormous clawed feet.

"Rantu! Rantu!" scream the mushroom men in terror. They turn and run away.

"What does Rantu mean?" you wonder aloud.

"It's the monster who eats the mushrooms," says Quentin. "And although I have never seen it, its presence does seem a good reason for turning back."

"Quentin, if we're going to get out of here, we're going to have to take a few risks. If we're careful, the Rantu won't ever see us."

"I wonder if this Rantu eats birds," Owl chirps thoughtfully.

Moving quietly, the four of you follow Fox out of the cavern. The corridor you enter is most unusual, nearly twenty feet high and almost as wide. The same kind of silvery streaks in the walls of the corridor light your way. A spring of cold, clear water pours out of the wall and cascades down the corridor in the direction you're going.

You trudge onward, keeping alert, watching for the dreaded Rantu.

"Gosh, it's warm," complains Fox. "Maybe a drink of water will help."

"It is getting warm in here," says Quentin, loosening his shirt.

"Yowll!" screeches Fox, jumping back from the stream and rubbing his nose in anguish. "My node! My node!" And even as you watch, Fox's nose puffs to twice its normal size. "Da stream! Da stream! Id's hod!" barks Fox.

Quickly you open your pouch and bring out a small jar of healing lotion. Tucking Fox under your arm, you pour it on his nose.

"Ow! You're killig me! Don't ged id in my eyes!" shrills Fox. But soon the healing lotion works its magic and Fox's cries turn to whimpers. "Carry me," he whines.

"I can't, Fox. It's too dangerous. I need my hands free in case we meet the Rantu. You'll have to walk." Hardening yourself to his pitiful cries, you move on.

Soon it is obvious to all that the corridor is growing hotter. The stream sizzles and steams and the silvery lines in walls turn a dull glowing red.

At last you come to a bend in the path. A screen of glowing stalactites prevents you from seeing what lies beyond, but you hear a strange noise that goes Splut! Splut! Splut!

Heat rises in waves around you and the walls shimmer as though they were mirages.

Grasping your dagger, you slip around the

screen and gape. A large crystal room soars above you, throbbing with a deep-red glow. Sand crunches underfoot as you walk forward and see a volcanic vent rising from the floor. Splut! Splut! gurgles the lava as it simmers.

Cradled on the red-hot lava are five huge eggs, each a different color—crimson, lime, royal blue, emerald, and apricot.

Listening carefully, you hear a clicking, chipping noise as though something inside an egg were trying to get out. Shielding your face from the terrible heat, you stare down at the enormous eggs.

"What do you think that noise is?"

"It must be a baby Rantu trying to get out," answers Quentin. "We should kill it."

Holding your dagger at the ready, you wait for the monster to hatch.

The royal-blue egg rocks from side to side. Then a tiny crack appears on the shell. Another blow and the crack widens! Still another, and a tiny sharp horn breaks through the shell. It seems to rest for a moment, then it attacks the shell with renewed energy until a hole the size of your head is made.

You are very curious, more curious than afraid. But you remind yourself that you are watching the birth of a dreaded Rantu, and you steel yourself for a death blow.

Then two tiny scaly blue jaws seize a chunk of shell and crunch it to dust.

You creep closer, but the inside of the egg is so dark that you cannot see anything.

Two big blue eyes with gold centers and fringed with thick lashes stare out at you. And the Rantu, never taking its eyes from your face, pushes its head free of the shell.

Spellbound, you stare into its eyes.

"Kill it!" cries Quentin.

"Run, Jaimie!" cry Fox and Owl.

But your friends' cries are like the wind as you stare at the creature before you.

There is great intelligence and love in the eyes of the Rantu. A great yearning for something you never even knew you lacked fills your chest. And love flows from you to the Rantu, who accepts it without question.

Haltingly you reach out, ignoring the terrible heat, and break away the shell.

The shell crumbles and there, floating on a pool of lava, is a baby dragon. Royal blue from the tip of its egg tooth to the last perfect shining scale, the dragon flutters its wet wings and steps out of the lava.

"Retreat!" begs Owl. But you stand fast.

And the dragon unfurls its gauzy blue wings, lifts hesitantly into the air, lands in your waiting arms, and sighs, "Mama," in a tiny, whispery voice.

Staggering, you step back until you reach level ground, where you sink to the sand.

"Why didn't you kill it, Jaimie? It's a baby Rantu! Put it down. I'll kill it!" shouts Quentin, raising his sword high.

"No!" you yell, raising your dagger to ward off the blow. The baby huddles in your lap and screams a long plaintive wail that echoes throughout the cavern.

A terrible rumble shakes the cave. Then the far side of the lava pool erupts, spewing molten rock everywhere.

Rising out of the pool, looming larger and larger with every passing second, is the largest, most terrifying dragon in the whole world. Molten rock drips off its head and slithers down maroon scales. Eyes sparking with rage, the dragon pauses as it spots the broken egg. Trumpeting, it turns, and time stops. You and Quentin freeze in fear with weapons raised and the baby dragon clutched to your breast. You have never been so frightened in all your life. You wish you knew how to disappear.

Then, rage fades from the dragon's eyes and it says, "Release my child unharmed and I will grant you anything you desire."

"Harm him? I wouldn't harm him. I was trying to help him. Please don't hurt US! All we want is to get out of here. And of course, we'll give you back your baby," you stammer.

But saying is easier than doing. The baby dragon clings tightly to your tunic, burying its muzzle in your neck, squealing loudly when you try to pry it loose.

"You seem to have charmed the young prince," says the maroon dragon. "I don't understand it, but Rainbow Dragons are never wrong. If the prince has chosen you, you must be honorable in spite of the appearance of

things. Please tell me your story while we try to convince the prince to let go."

Taking a deep breath, you try to steady your shaking voice as you tell the dragon the whole strange story. As you speak the names of the wizards, the dragon grows enraged.

"Malus, Pothos, Rubus! Hated names! Because of them I hide in dark caves, far from the light of day. Once, Rainbow Dragons were all-powerful and ruled wisely and well with King Chromos. But after Chromos died, there was no one strong enough to take his throne, and the hated wizards claimed Rainbow Castle as their own. Against their evil, we were helpless without a human to channel our power, and we had to flee the earth. Most of us took to the clouds. I, Maroon II, wife of King Cobalt, have remained here, in the depths of Rainbow Castle, waiting for the last of our children to hatch."

"Well, now that they're hatching, can't you leave?" you ask.

"And go where? None of us will be free until the legend comes to pass."

"Legend? What legend?" asks Fox.

"The legend tells of one who will arrive out of darkness and win the love of the King of the Rainbow Dragons. On that day, good will triumph. But that has not happened," sighs Maroon, "and evil still reigns."

"But your majesty, your queenliness, didn't you say this little fellow was a prince?" asks Fox.

"Yes. Royal Blue is the son of Cobalt, King of the Rainbow Dragons. He is the prince, heir apparent to the throne. And if the legends are true, he will be king one day."

"Your Majesty, may I suggest that Jaimie arrived out of the darkness. And it certainly seems that the prince loves him," says Fox.

All eyes fall to your lap, where young Royal Blue lies curled in a tight ball around your hand, purring deeply in his sleep.

"Could it be true? Could you be the heir of legend? Could our time of darkness and despair be over?" cries Maroon.

Enfolding you and Royal Blue in her wings, she says, "The legends never lie. The time of salvation is at hand. The wizards have grown fat and lazy. They no longer count us as enemies to fear. We shall teach them that they are wrong. I shall send a rainbow message to all my kindred and soon the evil wizards will be overthrown, and the Rainbow Dragons shall reign once more."

Clutching you gently to her chest, the huge dragon looks down at you and the slumbering baby and smiles.

THE END

You grasp the edge of the door and pull. Your fingers seem to slip through the edge of the door, but the door itself does not move.

"Look at this!" you exclaim, moving your fingers through the door's edge. "Maybe we can just walk right through the door!" Without hesitating, you walk straight ahead.

Clonk! Very real pain spreads through your nose.

"Ow! that hurt!"

"Well, cross that off," says Fox with a grin.

"Nothing ventured, nothing gained," mutters Owl.

"Well, I guess that puts us back to square one," you say sadly, rubbing your sore nose. All the while, the thin, high-pitched noise continues.

Please turn back to page 48
and make another choice.

"We accept your challenge, gentlemen," says Pentegarn.

"Excellent," hisses Rubus. "These are the rules. No magical items may be used. Your staff, ring, and cube must be set aside. And we will remove all of our special aids."

As he speaks, a variety of rings, charms, and necklaces clatter to the floor.

"Any magic, so long as it is performed by your skills alone, is allowed."

"How do we know you're not hiding something special?" you ask.

"Would we do that?" protests Pothos.

"Do owls fly?" sneers Fox.

"Any other rules?" asks Pentegarn.

"No. It's very simple," replies Pothos. "The four of us go into the Great Hall and whoever emerges alive wins."

"The three of you against Pentegarn! That's not fair!" you exclaim.

"Fair? Fair? Of course it's fair! Your precious Pentegarn studied under the Great Gump. We had to settle for the lowly Scrumbog. And we learned things only when we could wake him up or keep him from getting drunk. And you forget that Pentegarn's at least three hundred years older than we are. He's had all that time to practice and acquire new knowledge. It will take everything we three know to make it fair. But we have a few tricks up our sleeves."

"Don't worry, Jaimie," says Pentegarn. "Everything will be just fine."

"Don't be so sure of that," sneers Malus.

"Well, now, there's no reason to wait. Let's begin," says Pentegarn, striding toward the door. You trail after him uncertainly.

"Halt!" screeches Rubus. "Where do you think you're going? No one goes into that room except us. The zoo stays outside!"

"Just give me the word, kid, and I'll bite him," snarls Fox.

"The fellow is correct, Jaimie," says Owl. "The contest is not ours. We must not intrude."

"But what shall we do?" you exclaim angrily. "I can't just sit around here and twiddle my thumbs."

"No, indeed," says Malus. "We would like to know that you will not be twiddling—or meddling!—while we are occupied."

"What do you suggest?" asks Pentegarn.

"We have several suggestions," says Rubus, rubbing his hands together.

1) "You can go to Limbo. It's very nice at this time of year." Turn to page 139.

2) "You can rest in the tower. The view is quite nice." Turn to page 136.

3) "You can relax in our game room in the basement." Turn to page 33.

"It's so hard to know what to do," you mutter, pressing both hands to your head.

"Maybe if I become wise, I'll know what to do and how best to do it."

Placing your finger on the first word of the "Be Wise" spell, you begin to read hesitantly. As you reach the last magic word, you look around you one last time, and then speak the final word.

There is a wispy puff of smoke . . . and nothing happens! Sighing, you start to take your finger off the page when you notice that it seems old and wrinkled! How can this be? Snatching your hand from the book, you hold it in front of your eyes and see skin, loose with age, fragile, delicate bones, and long yellow fingernails.

"Do you give up yet?" asks a quavery voice, cracked with age.

Turning, you see Fox, white with silver frosting his beautiful coat, still sitting on top of the dictionary. One white wing waves feebly from between its closed pages.

"E equals MC squared!" you say.

"What's that?" shouts Fox. "Speak up!"

"I am uncertain as to the exact importance of the equation, but I have no doubt that it is both wise and full of immense meaning," you say carefully.

"Oh, no!" wails Fox. "What have I done to deserve two of you?"

THE END

"You'll like the tower. It's pleasant at this time of the year," says Malus with a nasty smile.

"I guess that sounds all right," you say.

Too late you see Pentegarn's look of dismay. But before you can speak, there is a blinding light, a clap of thunder, a great wind . . . and then nothing.

Slowly your eyes open. Lying beside you on a hard floor are Fox and Owl. You sit up quickly and gather their silent forms to your chest. "Fox! Owl! Speak to me!"

"Somebody get that giant," croaks Fox.

"What giant?"

"The giant who stepped on me," moans Fox.

"As usual, you exaggerate," says Owl, blinking blearily. "It was no giant, it was magic. We have been tricked by those wizards. Where are we?"

You are in a small round stone room. In front of you is a tall, narrow window with cold wind and rain blowing in. Looking around, you see a threadbare carpet, a heavy wooden door, and an empty stone fireplace. Nothing else.

"Wonderful. 'The tower is pleasant this time of the year,'" mimics Fox, shivering inside his thick coat of red fur. "What now, kid? Do something before we freeze to death."

"Perhaps we should first do something about the spiders," says Owl.

"Spiders? What spiders?" you ask, looking about wildly in panic.

Owl points upward with his wing and says, "Those spiders."

Coming down from the ceiling are at least two dozen large, nasty-looking spiders.

"Do something!" screeches Fox. "They look poisonous!"

1) "I could eat them," suggests Owl. "They won't hurt me." Turn to page 52.

2) "I could squash them as they fall," you say. Turn to page 149.

3) "Don't touch them!" cries Fox. "Use a magic spell." Turn to page 67.

There is a sudden Poof! a bright white light, and a feeling of weightlessness.

"Fox! Owl! Where are you?" you yell in panic from the depths of a pink fog.

"Yip! Yip! Yip!" you hear Fox scream.

"I fear we have a problem, young one," says Owl as he flaps down through the pink cloud and lands gently on your shoulder.

"Where are we?" you say, floundering in a soft, pink cottony substance.

"I fear we have been deceived," sighs Owl. "Limbo is not the name of a geographic location on earth. It's a state of being. Limbo means 'far away from anywhere that matters.' It's total helplessness."

Please turn to page 69.

As you move around the edge of the castle, you hear the peculiar noise a little more clearly. It's almost like screeching. You see many windows, but they are too high and too narrow to think about entering. Even the windows nearest you are out of reach. You stand a while in deep thought.

"Listen, Owl," you say suddenly. "If you help, I bet we can get in one of the lowest windows. Here, grab Fox's tail and we'll see if you and I can move him through that window."

"I'm not sure I like this idea," mutters Fox.

"You want to stay here forever and eat clouds?"

"OK, I'm convinced, but be careful."

Owl grasps Fox's tail in his claws and, beating his wings, rises slowly. Thinking hard, you concentrate on helping raise Fox. Slowly he rises up into the air and hovers about ten feet up, his tail clenched between Owl's powerful talons. Gradually, you move Fox and Owl on a straight line toward the nearest open window.

Bonk! A solid thud. As your eyes widen in dismay, you lose your concentration, and watch in horror as Fox and Owl plunge to the ground.

For a moment, all is silent. Then there is a thrashing of wings, limbs, tails, and beaks, and a very angry and tousled Fox and Owl glare at you.

"Look, I'm sorry. Really I am. All I did was misjudge slightly. So I missed the window.

Remember, I'm just learning. Anyone can make a mistake, right?"

"Not with my body," growls Fox.

"I NEVER make mistakes," says Owl smugly.

"Well, I'm sorry. It was an accident. I promise I'll be more careful next time."

"Where have I heard that before?" mutters Fox. But you finally convince him to trust you. By concentrating very hard and watching carefully, you are able to get Fox through the window.

Then Owl comes back to help you. Although it is harder to do, you manage to levitate yourself through the window. All three of you lie on the floor inside the castle and recover from your efforts. Only a little light comes in through the narrow windows. The origin of the noise must be closer now, because it is much louder.

"I wonder what that horrible noise is!" you gasp.

"Probably a terrible monster that will eat us!" Fox groans. "And I'm so sore, I won't even care."

"Well, even-tempered as I am, it's even getting on my nerves," says Owl.

"Try to ignore it," you say, getting to your feet. "Let's find out what else is here."

"My superior vision tells me that there's nothing of importance to be found on this level. There's only a table piled with food and drink," reports Owl.

"ONLY food and drink? Let me at it," cries Fox, leaping past you.

You grab his wriggling body and hold him with great difficulty. "Wait a minute, Fox. Think! Eating and drinking in a strange place can be dangerous."

"So can NOT eating and drinking," says Fox, slipping through your hands and jumping on top of the table.

"Just wait one minute, Fox, just one. Let's look carefully for traps. Why would food and drink be placed upon a table in the middle of an empty room?"

The table, a delicate work of gold and silver covered with a crisp white lace tablecloth, seems quite normal. It holds a place setting for one. Cookies, cakes, candy, ice cream, and drinks fill the table.

"Looks good to me," barks Fox. "Big decision—eat it or not."

1) If you want to eat and drink the treats on the table, turn to page 42.

2) If you decide not to eat and drink anything, turn to page 118.

Fox sniffs the ground all around the room and then says, "Let's go down this passage."

"No! That is forbidden," says a mushroom man, shrinking back in fear.

"Why is it forbidden?" you ask.

"The Rantu," grunts the creature. "We bring fresh mushrooms and leave them at the feeding place. When they are gone we bring more. Not allowed to go farther."

"Fox, why do you want to go down this passage? Are you sure it's the right way?"

Muzzle lifted, Fox tests the air once more. "I'm sure it's the right way. That other passage just smells musty. This one smells funny, kinda hot somehow. And I smell a strange animal, but I also smell fresh air."

1) If you decide you don't want to meet a monster named Rantu in a dark passageway, take the other route and try to follow the homing bat. Turn to page 106.

2) If you decide to follow Fox's instincts, turn to page 123.

"We can't leave Fox. I won't leave him with those monsters!" you say stubbornly.

Closing your eyes, you wish that somehow your spell would work the way you want it to. You are rewarded by Owl saying, "Well, you've done something, Jaimie, but I'm not sure what good it will do us."

The army of metal men hovers a foot above the ground. But still they advance, swinging their weapons before them.

"I wish they would all just fall down in a big scrap heap!" you say.

No sooner are the words out of your mouth than the metal figures collapse on the stone floor in a pile of disjointed arms and legs.

"Wow! How did that happen?" you ask in amazement. "I've never done anything like that before! But I sure am glad I did. That should fix them for a while!" Your voice rings with triumph. But seconds later a cold band of steel circles your ankle and begins to pull.

"Help! Owl, one of them has me!" The hand gives another powerful jerk, and you crash to the ground. You are being dragged closer to the mound of metal bodies.

"I cannot do anything, Jaimie! You must save yourself!" Closing your eyes, you clear your mind, picture the effect you wish, and then speak the spell Pentegarn used.

Instantly the metal hand releases its grip on your ankle and you scramble to your feet.

"Magnificent! I applaud you!" cries Owl.

You open your eyes in wonder.

Armored warriors still surround you, but now they are only six inches tall and their weapons are even tinier. The miniature army marches around the floor in all directions.

Even as you watch, two little figures bump into each other and begin to hack and slash at each other. Small sounds of clanging metal echo through the hall as the tiny figures bash at each other.

You smile with pleasure and then begin to laugh as you locate Fox. He lies on his back, all four feet in the air, seemingly dead, but with one open eye carefully viewing the scene.

"Fox! I thought you were dead."

"I may be, kid. I'm afraid to move and find out," says Fox out of the corner of his mouth. Just then a small suit of chain mail marches up to Fox and climbs up his shaggy side. Standing on the red, furry chest, the little figure pulls out a battle axe and waves it above its head, taking aim.

"That does it," barks Fox. Leaping to his feet, he grasps the metal man by its head, shakes it violently, and tosses it across the room where it lands with a clink.

Staggering slightly, Fox swaggers up to you. A long bloody gash creases an eyebrow.

"Oh, Fox, you're bleeding!"

"Better bleeding than dead, kid."

Quickly you tear a portion of your tunic off and wrap it around Fox's head.

"Great! Do I look distinguished?"

"I think we can say that you have acquired

a certain style that you previously lacked," answers Owl.

"Let's leave," you say nervously. "I don't know how long this spell will last."

Threading your way through the tiny army, you sidestep many battles.

"You know, I don't understand why that spell worked without being renewed. I already used the levitation spell once today. And how come it worked on all those guys at once? Usually a spell works on only one thing at a time. It could NEVER work on a whole army! Even Pentegarn couldn't do that."

"Must be magic, kid," says Fox jokingly. "Maybe you got yourself a wish ring."

"Do you think so?" you ask, raising your finger and staring at the ring.

"Make another wish and see," suggests Fox.

"But the problem is, there are two kinds of wish rings—one grants only three wishes and one grants many. If this one grants only three, a fourth wish might undo the first three and we'll be in a real mess."

1) If you decide to wish on the ring, turn to page 71.

2) If you decide not to take a chance on the ring again, turn to page 24.

As the first round black body falls, you slice its silky thread and step on it.

"This won't take any time at all," you say, and for the next few minutes you slice threads and crush spiders without stopping. Then, you notice that there seem to be more spiders than you realized. You move faster and faster, but the spiders drop even more quickly and in ever-growing numbers.

Suddenly you feel a sharp sting on your neck. Ignoring the pain, you continue killing spiders until you realize that you are slowing down, like a machine grinding to a halt. Slower and slower you move. Your arm is almost too heavy to lift. In fact, your whole body is heavy and tired. Maybe you'll lie down for a second. Then, later, you'll get up and fight some more.

You sink to the floor, ignoring Fox and Owl's screams, and fall into a deep sleep. Instantly the spiders swarm over you and begin weaving a cozy form-fitting cocoon of soft silk around your body.

"What do we do now, Featherface? We'd better do something or the kid's a goner."

"I don't know," says Owl. "I shall have to ponder this problem."

"Well, ponder fast or we're finished," says Fox nervously as he views a new army of spiders gathering on the ceiling.

THE END

Sheathing your dagger, you call out, "Hello. We come in peace. May we approach?"

A soft voice answers, "If you are friends and come in peace, you may enter."

Cautiously you enter the cave and then stop, stunned by brilliant bursts of color. Slowly, your vision clears and you wish it had not. Before you looms a huge dragon. Lowering its head till it is level with your own, it says, "Why have you come, human? Do you seek to harm us or steal our colors? Be warned, if that is your intent."

"We come in peace. We are here against our will and wish only to return to our own world."

"How come you to the cloud world?" asks the dragon.

Quickly, you outline the events that have led to your present troubles.

"Malus! Pothos! Rubus! Hated names! Evil persons!" says the dragon, angrily. "Let me show you what they have done!" Turning gracefully, it leads you into the depths of the cave. You pass three nests woven of soft mist and a sprinkle of stars and stop at the far end of the cave. Shielding your eyes against the bright glow, you stare in awe at mounds of pure color.

"Horizon Blue, Storm Green, Moon Orange, Sun Gold, Dusk Purple, Twilight Indigo, Radiant Red—all the colors of the rainbow, all carefully harvested by us when they are in their prime. After a storm we gather up a selection of each and blow a rainbow across the sky. It is our mission in life. Without us and others of our kind, there would be no rainbows. Should we vanish from the earth, there would be less beauty in the world, and when beauty dies, evil takes its place.

"Until recently, only a few hundred years ago, we lived on earth, in Rainbow Castle, our ancestral home, with the great wizard Chromos. But Chromos died and no one was found to succeed him.

"Greed, evil, and war tore at the kingdom, and Malus, Pothos, and Rubus came to Rainbow Castle and declared war upon us.

"They used their magic and before we could protect ourselves, they had killed most of us, including Cobalt, my brother, King of the Rainbow Dragons."

Crystal tears tremble on the dragon's lashes. "Somehow, we three escaped and made our home here in the cloud caves, but even now we are not safe. Lately, Malus, Pothos, and Rubus have been creeping in while we are out gathering colors, and stealing from us. They believe that they can change the colors into gems. Each time they fail, they return and steal more. Fools that they are, they do not realize that a rainbow is more precious, rare, and beautiful than any earthly gem.

"The last time they were here, we returned and caught them in their thievery. In their panic to escape, they threw a spear that almost hit Vermillion. Topaz chased them, but they got away."

Scales heaving with emotion, the dragon fans herself with one large wing. "Oh, dear! If I allow my anger and grief to become hatred, I will sink to their level and be no better than they."

Calming herself, the dragon adds, "You must think me terribly rude. Where are my manners? I am Ultramarine and these are my children, Topaz and Vermillion. Please excuse my outburst, but those wizards have caused us so much grief!"

"Maybe my friends and I can help," you say. "If we could get back to earth, we'd stop them somehow."

"Getting to earth is simple," says Topaz.

"Topaz, can we blow a rainbow bridge?"

"Well, they're hard, keeping the colors all together, but if Vermillion helps . . . maybe."

The littlest dragon peeks at you over the edge of her mother's gauzy wing. Meeting your eyes, she withdraws quickly, a bright blush flooding the scales of her head.

"Vermillion, stop this nonsense. We need your help. Come out and behave!" And using a wing and her mouth, the dragon mother gently pushes a blushing Vermillion forward.

"Now, listen closely. This is what we have to do," and the largest dragon talks for a long time.

As the day draws to an end, Ultramarine rises to her feet and says, "Now, remember all I've told you, especially what to do if Pentegarn has been harmed. We might be able to

save him, but only if we work together."

"Madam, your words are engraved on my heart," says Owl, bowing over a taloned hand.

Flustered, the dragon says, "Come now, children. We must blow a nice sturdy bridge."

Placing themselves before the piles of color, the dragons drink deeply until their cheeks bulge. Then, returning to the mouth of the cave, they begin to sway back and forth. And a soft, melodic humming, like the sound of sun shining in the rain, thrums from their lips. Wisps of color drift from Topaz and weave back and forth between strands of dew-drenched mist blown by Vermillion. Mingling with and binding their colors are those of their mother.

At last, hollow-cheeked and flushed with effort, the dragons sit back on their haunches and smile gently at each other.

You quickly step up to Vermillion, before she can hide, and kiss her on the cheek. A brilliant red glow covers her scales.

"Don't you think we should get going?" Fox asks nervously.

"Fox is right," says Ultramarine. "You must hurry. These bridges are very short lived. Now remember all I've told you."

Although the bridge looks fragile and shaky, it actually feels quite strong. Slipping first on a bit of red, sliding now on a band of green, you clamber down the bridge, crossing at last from sky to earth. As your feet touch the ground, the bridge begins to break up and disappear. Within seconds, nothing remains but a few shreds of rainbow-studded mist and a sparkling rainbow scale at your feet. You pick it up quickly and hide it in your pocket. Then, before your courage can fail, you enter Rainbow Castle.

Halls stand empty and silent, and no one appears. Striding to the giant double doors of the Great Hall, you grasp the handles and open the doors wide.

Pentagarn lies on the floor as though dead. Above him, holding magical devices in their hands, are the three wizards.

"You cheated!" you shriek, outraged.

The wizards scream in protest at the sight of you, but the three of you ignore them and rush to Pentegarn's side.

"Thank the gods he's still alive! Quick, Owl, Fox, we must do as Ultramarine said."

Ignoring the threats of the wizards, you grasp your two friends and concentrate on covering Pentegarn with thoughts of caring and love.

Instantly the wizards' shouts fade to the buzz of mosquitoes on a summer's eve. A thick beam of radiant rainbow appears over your head. The shafts of pure color pour down upon you, bathing you in their brilliance and outlining you in gold.

Suddenly, the line begins to waver and fade. "Concentrate!" you yell.

The line grows stronger and holds firm. Slowly, like thunder fading into the distance,

the colors dim and disappear. Pentegarn stirs. You help him to his feet.

"The wizards broke their word and used magic amulets. Where are they?" he asks.

Turning, you look around the empty hall and see nothing but three mounds of color—red, blue, and yellow.

Then, even as you watch, the colors spin themselves into thin, wispy threads and slowly waft upward, disappearing.

"They really did it!" you say in awe.

"Who did what?" groans Pentegarn, clutching his head.

"The dragons! They reduced Malus, Pothos, and Rubus to their primary colors. Hurry, let's go outside!"

Bursting through the castle doors you look up into the sky. And there, arching across the heavens, is an enormous rainbow, more beautiful than you dreamed possible.

"There they are," you whisper. "Do you think it's so beautiful because something so evil is being used for good?"

"I think I missed something," says Pentegarn, scratching his head.

"Don't worry. I'll tell you all about it," says Fox. "I was great."

THE END

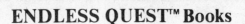

ENDLESS QUEST™ Books

Ask for these exciting DUNGEONS & DRAGONS™ titles at better bookstores and hobby shops everywhere!

#1 DUNGEON OF DREAD
You are a fighter in quest of treasure, willing to challenge the evil wizard in his mountain hideaway. Only by quick thinking and action will you emerge safely from the Dungeons of Dread.

#2 MOUNTAIN OF MIRRORS
An elven warrior hoping to keep your village from starving, you must enter the mysterious Mountain of Mirrors to fight monsters who have been stealing caravans of food.

#3 PILLARS OF PENTEGARN
You and your friends, Fox and Owl, journey into the ruins of Castle Pentegarn. You join three adventurers who are after the powerful Staff of Kings.

#4 RETURN TO BROOKMERE
You are an elven prince who must return to the ruins of the family castle, Brookmere, and learn what evil lurks there. Only courage and cleverness will bring you out.

#5 REVOLT OF THE DWARVES
The dwarves who once served your kingdom have revolted. You and your family are the first humans to be captured. But you escape! You must warn the prince and save your family.

#6 REVENGE OF THE RAINBOW DRAGONS
You are Jaimie, wizard apprentice to Pentegarn, on quest to Rainbow Castle to meet the challenge of three evil wizards. You must use wits and courage to save yourself.

For a free catalog write:
TSR Hobbies, Inc.
POB 756 Dept. EQB
Lake Geneva, WI 53147